BIZ-OP:
How to Get Rich with
"Business Opportunity"
Frauds and Scams

by Bruce Easley

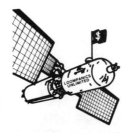

Loompanics Unlimited
Port Townsend, Washington

BIZ-OP: How to Get Rich with "Business Opportunity" Frauds and Scams
© 1994 by Bruce Easley

Cover by Daniel Wend/MEDIA Graphics

Illustrations by Mary Ellen Smith
Photos by Bob Jenks

Published by:
Loompanics Unlimited
P.O. Box 1197
Port Townsend, WA 98368
Loompanics Unlimited is a division of Loompanics Enterprises, Inc.

ISBN 1-55950-109-X
Library of Congress Catalog Card Number 94-75058

Contents

◆　◆　◆　◆　◆　◆　◆　◆　◆

Chapter 1:
Introduction To
Business Opportunity
Marketing And Locating

◆ ◆ ◆ ◆ ◆ ◆ ◆ ◆ ◆

Making money in business opportunity marketing is a lucrative racket that few people are familiar with. It came into being with the creation of newsprint. The first ads dealt with cure-alls, elixirs and miracle gadgets that did everything. The ads enticed with the same ploy that is being used today, appealing to greed: "Become a distributor of my product and get rich."

The basic concept has changed little. If a biz-opper in 1807 made you an exclusive distributor of an elixir, he could easily side-step you by putting a new label on his existing elixir bottle. The biz-opper could now set up another distributorship in the same area.

Today's vending machine biz-op operators use the same approach. They either change charities or sell a slightly different vending machine. Regardless, they give each "mooch" (customer) a guaranteed area.

This book, **Biz-Op**, contains all the necessary data you need to change your lifestyle. As long as you can follow instructions, you will quickly find yourself in an upper income bracket. Making money in biz-op marketing is inexpensive and simple. A first time biz-op operator can get started for under $900. The main theme of biz-op marketing is to show the public how to make money off your product.

There is nothing complex about getting a mooch to send you five grand. You only have to do six things:

◆ Find a product. A product can be almost anything. Charity honor boxes, gas additives, toys, vending machines, seeds, etc. The trick is not paying for the product until a mooch gives you a deposit. This is called the "Sell Before You Buy Method." In other words, you get the mooch's money before you buy the product.

◆ Advertise. (Place ads in out of state papers only. Never make a mess in your own backyard.) By following my successful ads you will receive a barrage of phone calls. (Included are copies of a variety of ads relating to different products.)

- Put together a biz-op profit pamphlet. (This book contains my complete million dollar marketing pamphlet. It is a proven winner.)
- Organize singers (endorsers). For singers, you only need friends or relatives who want to make money.
- Collect money. If you follow my step-by-step procedure, you will find yourself with a line of hot cash-toting mooches.
- Locate. (You will be taught the fine art of locating — the last step in the biz-op con.)

Reader, you are about to enter into a money-making world that very few people know about. By using my biz-op marketing system you will pocket more money than you ever dreamed possible.

When you are through with this book you can, if you choose, become part of a small group of people who have become wealthy off biz-op marketing.

Chapter 2:
Biz-Op Start-Up Cost

◆ ◆ ◆ ◆ ◆ ◆ ◆ ◆ ◆

The best part of getting into a biz-op operation (besides making money) is the start-up cost. It is almost nothing compared to a standard business. Biz-op marketing is not a "track record," goodwill type of business that you sell after years of hard work. This is a creative cash racket that is put together to make quick "hit and run," underground money. What I intend to do is show you how to get started making instant money without spending big bucks.

Most people who are considering a business have excess money to invest. They are ready to bankroll their project. Many big buck spenders look at restaurants. Even a cheap, two-bit "mom and pop" will set you back 20 grand. A higher quality restaurant-bar combo is 150 Gs. A McDonald's franchise is one million.

If a person is into cars, he might consider a Minit Lube or Precision Tune. In this case, you are looking at a cool hundred thousand.

Your average biz-op investor does not fall into the big buck investor category. You will discover that 95% of your mooches will only have between $5,000 and $10,000 to invest. They expect you to get them a piece of the American dream pie for peanuts. In reality, that's what they will end up with, peanuts.

What makes going into business attractive? Independence? No one to answer to? Bullshit! Going into business is suicide. You are thrown into a sea of employees who will rip your heart out. Federal and state governments have their slimy tax hands in your pocket and you had better be a good customer ass kisser if you expect to survive. Franchisers expect you to conform to their rules and regulations and if you don't, God help you. When everything is said and done, business is a big headache. I know. I have had restaurants and several car rental agencies. Neither one of those businesses has come close to generating the income I am presently making. A good biz-op operator can pick up a quarter of a million yearly. (A lot of that is "hidden money.") A so-so operator can stick at least 60 grand in his pocket.

Biz-op marketing has very few of the problems that a regular business has. All of your customers (the mooches) will eventually hate you. You will never have a happy customer and you don't give a shit. You take their money, say good-bye and walk. The only employees you have are illegal singers. (See Chapter 5.) As long as you give them their agreed percentage, they are content. You have no employee taxes or medical insurance to pay. Federal taxes are not a problem. Since you are dealing in an all-cash business, it is easy to hide money from Uncle Sam. Franchise fees? The only fee is what you collect from the mooch. Sometimes you can actually collect an exclusive distributorship fee from a super gullible mooch.

Cost Of A Biz-Op Operation

To get started in this lucrative business, this is what is required:

- Business phone line run to an answering service – $50 set-up charge (one time only). Monthly fee $21.46 plus long distance service.
- A 1-800-number – $30 set-up (one time only). Monthly charge $6 plus line usage. (When you get a "mooch hit list," you will need another 1-800-number.)
- Answering service – Monthly fee $45.50 for 55 calls. The charge after 55 calls is 40 cents each. NEVER GIVE AN ANSWERING SERVICE YOUR HOME ADDRESS OR PHONE NUMBER! The fewer people who know where you are, the better. Give your mail box number as your mailing address.
- Business cards – $50 (needs to be a nice looking card).
- Two suits – Prices vary for men and women. My suits usually run about $300 each. You really don't need to purchase a suit until you get your first job deposit. I find it is easier to do locating in a suit. Store owners have more respect. It also makes a better impression on the mooch. If you do not have a nice looking car, I suggest you take some of the profit from your first deal and get one. If you have to tour a mooch in an older car, explain that your auto is in the shop and that the mechanic let you use his extra car. It's all part of the game – gold jewelry, nice car, suit. After all, if you have someone "hooked" for ten grand, you want to look as if you are successful. Don't worry about the car or jewelry until you have "bagged a mooch" or two.
- File cabinet, 2-drawer – It can be cardboard or metal. Just have a place to keep track of your mooch hit list. (A computer is nice if you have one.) A hit list can be sold to telemarketing services and sold in *USA Today*.
- PO Boxes (not federal), Mail Box, etc. – Six months rent, $35. You start with one PO Box, but after you get a mooch hit list you will need two. NEVER GIVE A MAIL BOX EMPLOYEE YOUR HOME ADDRESS OR PHONE NUMBER. Try to find a place that doesn't ask for your driver's license. If you cannot, pay someone to rent the box for you or use a false I.D.
- Cash on hand – $300. (Set up a D.B.A. checking account.) – Necessary for newspaper ads. Some papers will give you 30 days to pay. Those I usually string along for 90 days. Newspapers will not accept an out of state ad unless you pay for it first. Occasionally you will get a new person who will take your ad without realiz-

ing there is an out of state policy, but the majority of times, you had better have a check ready.

Total Set-Up Cost

Business phone, $50 set-up (one time), monthly flat fee $21.46.	$ 71.46
1-800-Number, $30 set-up (one time), monthly flat fee $6 plus line usage.	$ 36.00
Answering service:	$ 45.50
Business cards:	$ 50.00
Suit (optional):	$250.00
Cardboard file:	$ 10.00
Mail Box:	$ 35.00
Newspaper cash:	$300.00
TOTAL	$797.96

This is all the operating capital you need to get started.

Chapter 3:
Classified Ads

◆ ◆ ◆ ◆ ◆ ◆ ◆ ◆ ◆

I'm assuming most of my readers are new to biz-opping. If that is the case, then your experience in placing classified ads is limited. Here are some pointers for the beginner.

Be brief. Even though some of the ads you will read are more than four lines, it is still better to keep it to four or five lines. All the ads in this book have been "continuous runners" – ads that run in the paper week after week. That means they're making money. If you're not getting a response to your ad, check the newspaper first to make sure they haven't misworded your ad. I had a seed display ad that was worded "deed display." If everything is correct, then something is wrong and you need to rework your ad.

Start your ad with attractive bold type. The heading is THE MOST IMPORTANT PART OF YOUR AD. Examples:

EARN $1,000 A WEEK
$ PAY FAX $
BEST ALL CASH BUSINESS
LUCRATIVE
GROUND FLOOR OPPORTUNITY
EXCITING NEW PRODUCT

Make sure the reader gets excited enough to make the phone call.

To find a list of out-of-state newspapers (or in-state ones, too) go to a library and ask to see *Gale's Directory of Publications*. This guide lists all newspapers by their city and state of publication. It gives the newspaper's address, phone number, ad rates, and usually the name of the advertising manager. It also gives the newspaper's circulation.

Classified Discounts

When talking to the classified salesperson, declare yourself an in-house agency. This means you're creating the ads for your company instead of having an advertising agency do it. Standard discount for an in-house agency is 15 percent.

Pay in advance. Since you'll be paying cash for most of your ads, ask if there is a discount for paying cash. The majority of times, you'll receive a 5 to 10 percent discount.

If you're onto a good product and it appears you'll be running it for longer than four weeks, ask for a contract rate. The price of the ad will continue to drop the longer you run it. They will expect you to fulfill the contract (6-16 weeks), but if you're making good money, that will not be a problem.

Chapter 4:
Basic Phone Pitch Rules

◆ ◆ ◆ ◆ ◆ ◆ ◆ ◆ ◆

Biz-op phone pitch rules are quick and easy to follow. The object of the first phone pitch call is to get the mooch to accept your Fed-Ex package of information. You only need to give a brief sketch of your product. The main thing is, you fulfill the mooch's "greed factor." LET HIM KNOW HOW MUCH HE IS GOING TO MAKE.

Your second call is made after the mooch has his package. This call is known as the "singer set-up." Its main purpose is to give your mooch your singers' phone numbers.

Your third call back is the "urgent one." It is made after your singers contact you. They will give you a "mooch report" on whether he is "hot to trot" or still debating. On this call, you tell the mooch you have several other people who are looking at his area and that if he is still interested in making money you need a tentative answer. If he gives you an okay, but wants another day, tell him you will call him back within 48 hours.

The fourth call back is "the close." Time for the mooch to overnight a cashier's check. We will go over the phone pitch again in other chapters.

Answering Service

The answering service is the tool that opens the door to the mooch. Their job is to take your 1-800-number messages. They will also relay special instructions, such as quoting prices of "re-buy vends." (See Chapter 13.) Their job is mainly limited to getting you mooch numbers.

Chapter 5:
Singers And
Avoiding Phone Fraud

◆ ◆ ◆ ◆ ◆ ◆ ◆ ◆ ◆

Singers are illegal. The federal government looks upon them as perpetrators of interstate phone fraud.

A singer is usually a friend or relative who lives in another state. They earn their money by lying about the product you are selling. A singer only has samples of your product, but he will tell the mooch that he has 10 high-grossing stores that are handling it and he is considering purchasing enough product for 10 more stores. He tells the mooch that he is happy with his business and that at present is netting between $700 and $1,000 a week.

A singer is paid by units. If you sell a mooch 10 displays of skin cream, you pay your singer $200, or $20 a unit (providing the deal closes). The majority of times it is advisable to have two singers.

Your singer must have pictures of the displays, samples of the product, and the marketing pamphlet. He also needs a complete cost breakdown. If you are selling a mooch a bottle of skin lotion for $5 and its retail value is $15, less the store's 30 percent, the net would be $5.50. That means in order to have a $1,000 a week profit you need to move 200 bottles of skin lotion.

A singer's math must jibe. If he is unsure of the amount of a product he is moving it will jinx the sale. I always drill my singers with questions such as: "What kind of stores do you have the displays in?" "How much did you pay a locator to find the stores?" Money questions are important. Repeatedly ask your singer: "How did you pay for the product?" "Do you ever discount your product?" "How much are you making on each item?" If you have several products, the singer must have the net information on each one.

As I previously explained, singing is illegal. The federal government views it as interstate phone fraud, but there are ways you can beat this. One is to make sure your singers use a middle or fictitious name. NEVER LET THEM USE THEIR FULL NAME. After you have collected the mooch's money, pay to have your singer's phone number changed. The first time the phone company does it free. After that there is a

$10 charge. The number should always be unlisted. It then becomes almost impossible for a mooch to locate the singer. The only way he has of tracing the singer is through the disconnected phone number. If by some chance the mooch were to get the new number, all the singer has to do is deny he ever talked to the person. There is absolutely no way to prove otherwise. In all my years of operating, I have never known this to happen.

Another way of maneuvering around phone fraud is "the plant." A plant is a singer who has displays. If you are on to a good thing and have a lot of product to unload (as I did with Rain Forest displays) it pays to spend a little protective cash. When I set up the Rain Forest program I sent two singers 10 displays each and paid them $50 a unit to place them in different local stores. This eliminates the federal phone fraud rap. The government can no longer claim the singer is a decoy, because the singer has actual displays in retail outlets. A plant is good when you are dealing with a product that might gross $100,000 and take up to six months to move.

I still recommend, especially for the beginner, that you stay with a product you can "off" in 30 days. Quick "hit and run" money is the best and safest.

Chapter 6: Charities

◆ ◆ ◆ ◆ ◆ ◆ ◆ ◆ ◆

Charity products are mainly food vends, such as honor boxes and countertop vending machines. Originally countertop vending machines were installed on a percentage basis. The location was paid 10 percent of the machine's gross. After years of biz-op operators pushing vending machines, the market has become saturated. Now most biz-op operators "double-up a location" (place a machine in a location that already has one) by using a charity sympathy pitch.

My charity system is great for the first time biz-op operator. All the necessary charity contracts and locating forms are in this book. All you have to do is photocopy a charity contract and give it to your mooch. As long as the mooch sends in his contract and pays the monthly fees, the charities are happy.

Every charity has a fee for using its name. It averages between $1.50 and $3 a unit per month. Fifty honor boxes at $2 each would cost the mooch $100 a month. Most mooches, when they realize the projected profit sheet is bullshit (see marketing pamphlet), only pay once. Then, after weeks of disappointing sales, they take their honor boxes home and eat what's left.

If you read different charity contracts you will see the formats are similar. The same is true of the charity locating forms. Most charity contracts include a tax exempt number. When using a charity locating form, this number should be written at the bottom.

This tax number allows the mooch to deduct the amount he pays to the charity. The tax number also allows the location to deduct the amount it pays for rent on two square feet. The federal government considers the space the honor box or the vending machine takes up as a donation. The business is allowed to deduct that donated space as if it were a cash contribution. If a business is paying $10 a square foot for rent, it can deduct $20 a month. That's a total of $240 a year.

It always impresses the mooch when you give him that information.

Since you have copies of the charity agreements, you will not be dealing with the charity. The only name they will ever receive is that of your mooch.

Charity Locating

An average locator can put in 25 charity honor boxes or 10 vending machines a day. The charge to the mooch is $20 per honor box and $100 per vending machine. Your daily net will run between $500 and $1,000 a day.

Don't worry about the length of time a location keeps a product. It might only be there for a week. That's not your problem. Your job is to get rid of everything as quickly as possible. Naturally you do not tell the mooch this. He believes you are getting him good, solid, long lasting, money making locations. After all, he is paying top dollar for them.

When talking to a business remember two things: they do not like to make a long-term commitment and they may ask how much money goes toward the charity. There are three basic ways to overcome these problems. One, use your charity as a tool to create as much sympathy as you can. If I am placing honor boxes or vending machines for the National Federation of the Blind, I wear an eye patch. Two, always ask for the manager. Three, use the following pitch or a close variation of it. "Hello, my name is _____. I am working for the National Federation of the Blind and we are conducting our annual vending machine (or honor box) fund-raiser. The machines will be placed in your premises for 60 days (if it's an honor box, only two weeks) and all of the money goes toward our different rehabilitation programs. At the end of 60 days the machines will be removed. Last year we raised almost $200,000 and we are hoping to repeat that again this year. One of the nice things about our charity is that you get to eat your donation." *(That always gets a chuckle from the manager.)*

If you are placing a countertop vending machine you show the manager a picture of the machine, which you get from the manufacturer. When locating honor boxes carry them in with you. Most of the time the manager will let you leave it. You do not need a locating agreement for honor boxes, but remember to use the sign-off form (from the Appendix) and write down the name of the business, the manager's name, the address and the phone number.

Use the charity locating forms in the Appendix for vending machines only. The last sentence of the charity locating form is important. It relieves the location of any liability or continuing obligation. Most store owners want to make sure they are not liable for the vending machine. After pointing that out, tell the manager about the square footage tax write-off. Then hand the person a pen, get his signature, and split.

I work alone 90 percent of the time and use the National Federation of the Blind. The rest of the time I work with my son and use children's type of charities.

My son was the key when I hooked up with the American Association of Missing Children. With the cute kid in tow I would tell the location that my son at one time was missing and this organization found him. I now repay their kindness by volunteering once a year to place their charity vending machines.

My son and I also teamed up with the National Awareness Foundation ("Hugs not Drugs"). The pitch was, "We volunteered to help because my older son died of a drug overdose and we wanted to do our part to save other children." Of course that's all bullshit, but it worked quite well. My son, a nice looking, innocent kid, could soften the heart of even the most cold-blooded business person. Our success ratio was always way above average. One summer we did a job using the M.S. Society. We finished in record time by simply putting a leg brace on him.

Even though my son and I made a good team, I still find it easier to work with an eye patch than with another person.

When you have finished securing your charity locations you will need to collect the rest of your locating money.

If you are putting in charity honor boxes you just simply turn the location list (see Appendix) over to the mooch and collect what is due you. You do not tour mooches with charity honor boxes, but make sure all your addresses are correct.

Charity countertop vends are a different story. You will have to tour your mooch, but try to avoid taking him into the location. If you take the mooch in, the store owner might say, "This is only for 30 days. Right?" Your mooch, who is expecting his vending machine to stay in forever, will not want to hear that.

In order to prevent this I tell the mooch that I have explained to the location that a representative of the charity will be in to place the vending machine. "As far as the location is concerned, they believe the charity owns the machine not a private party. If I take you in and introduce you as the vending machine owner they will think something is strange. They are expecting a charity representative to place the vend, not a private vending machine owner. You are just the person that collects the money and fills the machine."

By telling the mooch this it alleviates the necessity of introducing him to the location owner. Instead of taking the mooch inside, you just point his locations out as you are driving by. Once you have finished the tour you turn the charity contracts over to the mooch and collect your money.

Chapter 7:
Marketing Pamphlet

◆ ◆ ◆ ◆ ◆ ◆ ◆ ◆ ◆

In this chapter I have laid out my complete marketing pamphlet. This is the same pamphlet that a mooch receives. The only necessary revamps will be inserting the name of your product and the restructuring of the profit sheet and location list. Those two must be tailored to meet the requirements of your product. Putting together a sales pamphlet is not complicated.

The pamphlet is a sales tool. It helps alleviate the mooch's fear of business by showing him how simple and profitable it is to handle the product you are selling.

Study this pamphlet carefully. You will use basically the same pamphlet, over and over, for every different product mentioned in this book: vending machines, work-at-home, greeting cards, phone and fax machines, etc. The pitch is always the same, only the name of the product and the numbers change. This is your mooch bait, so you have to learn how to dangle it in front of the mooch.

Capture The Untapped Market With Merchandise

Be a Distributor of an Incredible Product

A Product that has no competition

A Product that sells on sight

A Product that can be placed in a variety of retail stores

Own Your Own Business that...

◊ Produces year-round income

◊ Operates with a minimum of expense

◊ Requires no special skills to operate or service

◊ Products are compact, light, easy to handle

◊ No rent, utilities, or labor expenses to pay

◊ Does not require any service of mechanical equipment

◊ Excellent expansion and growth potential

Keys to Business Success

◊ No Employees

◊ Easy servicing

◊ Potential Growth

◊ Attractive Displays

◊ Tested Business Concept

◊ Security

◊ Low Overhead

◊ Multiple Sales

◊ Unique Product Line

◊ Good Profit & Pricing Structure

◊ Repeat Sales

◊ Reasonable Time Investment

◊ Company Support

We provide these necessary elements to create a fantastic business investment program. Our goal is to help the individuals who distribute our products to become prosperous in a business which is simple to operate AND is financially profitable.

By becoming a Distributor, you can share -at your local level- in the success brought about this unique Distributor network.

Sample 1

The first page (see Sample #1) gets the mooch's blood pounding. Phrases like "No Rent – No Employees – Repeat Sales" start his financial glands salivating. You will find the average "mooch" has never been in business and he will believe a great deal of what you tell him.

WORK FROM YOUR HOME

PART TIME • FULL TIME • OR ABSENTEE

- Easy Work!
- Set Your Own Hours!
- Work Full of Part time!

- No Selling!
- No Royalties!
- No Overhead!
- Immediate Income
- Huge Tax Advantages
- Fantastic Return on Your Investment

Unique Personalized Location System

Sample 2

The second page (see Sample #2) is the "be your own boss" page. Every mooch without exception wants to become independent and escape from his present job. "Easy Work – Set Your Own Hours – Huge Tax Advantage" are buzz words that light the mooch's fire. He wants a piece of the American Dream but his inexperience will turn his dream into a nightmare.

At the bottom of the page (see Sample #2) I use the phrase "Ground Floor Opportunity." I want the mooch to understand he is getting in on something new and will have exclusive territory.

Become a Distributor Today
Let   work for you!

Unlimited Retail Locations

The analysis of a retail store or business as a potenial location for your Display is very simple.

1. Does the business have good foot traffic?
2. Are children likely to be found on the premises, with their parents or alone?

If the answer to these questions is "YES", then that business has the potenial of being a good retail location, and it is highly likely that the operator is anxious for HIGH-IMPACT sales opportunities.

The following is a list of types of stores and businesses which have been successful locations for   Distributors.

- Amusement/Theme Parks
- Airports
- Auditoriums
- Baseball Card Stores
- Book Stores
- Bowling Alleys
- Bus Stations
- Cafes
- Camping Facilities
- Candy Stores
- Carnivals
- Car Washes
- Card & Party Shops
- Convenience Stores
- Children's Hospitals
- Civil Organizations
- Country Clubs
- Deli's

- Department Stores
- Discount Stores
- Drug Stores
- Expressway Oasis'
- Flea Markets
- Fairs
- Family Restaurants
- Fun Spots
- Gift Shops
- Grocery Stores
- Hardware Stores
- Hobby Stores
- Holiday Celebrations
- Hospital Gift Shops
- Hotel Gift Shops
- Interstate Car & Truck Stops
- Military Bases

- Novelty Stores
- Party Suppliers
- Pizza Parlors
- Recreation Centers
- Resorts
- Restaurants
- Shopping Centers
- Skating Rinks
- Street Festivals
- Souvenir Stands
- Sport Stores
- Tourist Attractions
- Tourist Service Stations
- Toy Stores
- Train Stations
- Truck Stops
- Variety Stores
- Video Stores

• CAN YOU THINK OF OTHERS?

Retail locations may be secured one of two ways; either through a professional location service or by the Distributor. If so desired,   will gladly furnish the names of professional location services to secure good retail locations for you.

Sample 3

The location page (see Sample #3) helps convince the mooch that there are enormous numbers of locations available for his product. It is important for the mooch to think that he will be able to get his product into the stores quickly.

The only major adjustments on Sample #3 will be the locations. If you are dealing with X-rated porn products many of these locations would be unsuitable. With a family-oriented product all of these locations could be used. The longer the list of locations the better the mooch likes it. The locations in Sample #3 are family places.

The Distribution Program

Make 'em an offer they can't refuse

The   Marketing Plan is very appealing to the prospective retailer. In the first place it enables them to retail proven successful products without any capital investment of their own. The retailer also doesn't have the worries of maintaining seperate inventories or the need to pay someone to keep the   display stocked. This puts you, the distributor, in a unique position of making an offer that any smart businessman cannot pass up, since it creaties an
"I CAN'T LOSE", situation for the store owner.

Slicing up the Pie

The retail outlets carrying
your   displays
will receive $1.00 for
each   sold,
your net profit is $1.25.
You may use our Toll Free Line or Fax number to re-order   All orders are quickly shipped to you UPS from our warehouse, within one week from receipt of the order, to assure your displays are kept full year round.

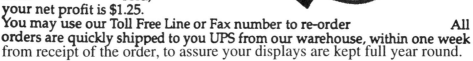

This fantastic program eliminates the need to inventory and store large quantities of   merchandise, and almost eliminates your overhead by reducing the need for such items as an office, employees, business telephone lines, warehouse space, special equipment and vehicles. The tax advantages to owning your own business can be impressive, so check with your accountant to determine your actual benefits.

Our 5 Step Distribution Plan is Simple!

1. Locate Retail Outlets For   *Displays*
2. Deliver and Set Up   *Displays*
3. Service Your   *Displays*
4. Reorder   *Inventory*
5. Count Your Money "$"!

What Could Be Easier?

Sample 4

The consignment page (see Sample #4) drives home the idea that all businesses want the mooch's product. They want the product because it's a "guaranteed sale." (The store just pays for what it sells.) The only thing the store has to give up is a little floor or counter space. In exchange they receive a percentage of the sales price.

All the mooch has to do is put his displays in, restock and collect money. What could be more simple? He makes money and the stores make money. Everyone is happy. His product could become a merchandising bonanza. Everyone knows of an overnight success story and everyone especially the mooch wants to become part of one. Only the mooch's story will not be a happy one.

PHENOMENAL TAX BENEFITS AND SAVINGS!

Are available to you as a Distributor, so you KEEP more of your business income.

IMPORTANT TAX INFORMATION

As a   Distributor, you may write off through depreciation the total purchase price of the equipment, usually over a period of 3-5 years. This benefit is also known as "Cost recovery".

In addition, and this is most important as it goes on and on,   Distributors are allowed tax deductions for expenses incurred in generating and collecting income and in operating and servicing the displays.

Besides direct expenses, the business portion of the following costs can be deducted from your gross income:

AUTO

Gas and Oil
Licenses
Insurance
Repairs
Depreciation

HOUSE

House payments or Rent
Taxes and Insurance
Electricity, Gas, Water
Repairs and Maintenance
Telephone
Depreciation (if owned)

KEOGH PLAN - TAX BONUS
Since you must own your own business to make this tax deduction (up to $30,000), this valuable tax savings is yours!

Sample 5

The tax page (see Sample #5) creates the illusion of the mooch making megabucks. You as the biz-op operator are looking out for the mooch's interest making sure he will net as much as possible off each dollar.

Tax jargon such as "Equipment Write-Offs" "Cost Recovery" and "Keogh Plan" plants the seed in the mooch's mind that you the biz-op operator understand his tax needs. Since the average mooch knows very little about taxes he appreciates that.

"I can't invest now"

AGE 18 - 25

I can't invest now, I'm too young! I'm still in school, you can't expect me to invest now. Besides, I'm young and I've got my whole life ahead of me. There is plenty of time to invest. Right?

AGE 25 TO 35

- You couldn't possibly expect me to invest now! I've only been in the workforce a few years. Things will be taking off soon and then I'll start thinking of investing. Anyway, I've still got a lot of time!

AGE 35 TO 45

- I can't invest now! I'm married and have a family to take care of. Wait till the kids are older, then I might start thinking about investing.

AGE 45 TO 55

- I'd like to invest now, but it's just not possible. I've got two children away at college and it takes everything I make just to keep them there. I've gone in debt the last couple years just to cover the college bills. But hopefully it won't last forever, then I'll start investing.

AGE 55 TO 65

- I should be investing right now, but money is too tight. It's hard for a man my age to get ahead. I wish I'd invested twenty years ago. Oh well, something might turn up. Who knows, I might win the lottery!

AGE OVER 65

- I guess it's too late now. We lost our home and now live with our daughter and her family. It's very awkward, but what else can we do? Who can live on Social Security? If only I'd invested when I had money.

No one Plans to Fail - But Most Fail to Plan

Let   **Provide you with the Financial Security you need for the Future!**

Sample 6

Pages 28 and 30 (see Sample #6 and Sample #7) are "Urgent Message" pages: "If you do not invest you will get old and your kids will have to feed you."

As you can see in Sample #6, each age group has a reason for not investing.

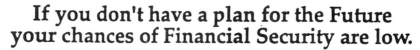

If you don't have a plan for the Future your chances of Financial Security are low.

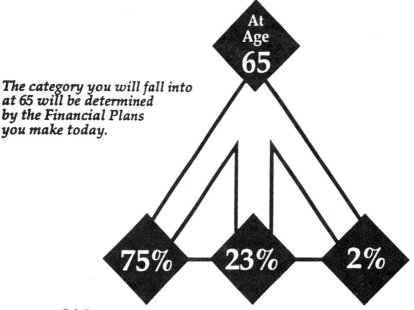

The category you will fall into at 65 will be determined by the Financial Plans you make today.

At Age 65

75% — Of the American People are dependant on relatives, friends and charity.

23% — Are still working.

2% — Are financially independent.

YOU NEED A PLAN FOR THE FUTURE
WHY?

According to the U.S. Department of Labor "Even in America only 1 person in 500 at age 65 will have as much as $24,000".

The Social Security Board reports "85 out of 100 reaching 65 do not possess as much as $250".

Why does this happen?

Because the Convenient Time to Save Money Never Comes!

It is estimated that of 100 individuals reaching age 65
- 45 may live to be 80
- 24 may live to be 85
- 10 may live to be 90

The Future will not Take Care of Itself, SO YOU MUST!

Let a _____ Distributorship be the financial decision you make today to provide for you family's security tomorrow!

Sample 7

Sample #7 includes government stats like: "85 out of 100 reaching 65 do not possess as much as $250.00;" and "Only one American in 500 will have as much as $24,000 when he reaches 65." The mooch doesn't want to become a government stat. He wants to become financially secure. He knows that a good business can and will give him the security he needs. All great entrepreneurs are gamblers and if he doesn't take a chance he may be denying his family a better life.

The pamphlet is a significant tool. In between your calls to the mooch, the pamphlet keeps his mind working. It is during this time that the mooch will call your singers. Your singers must have an identical pamphlet.

SALES / PROFIT POTENTIAL

LEVEL I   8 DISPLAYS

Sales/Day (per display)	Profit/Day	Profit/Week	Profit/Month	Profit/Year
4	40.00	280.00	1,204.00	14,448.00
6	60.00	420.00	1,806.00	21,672.00
8	80.00	560.00	2,408.00	28,896.00
12	120.00	840.00	3,612.00	43,344.00

LEVEL II   16 DISPLAYS

Sales/Day (per display)	Profit/Day	Profit/Week	Profit/Month	Profit/Year
4	80.00	560.00	2,408.00	28,896.00
6	120.00	840.00	3,612.00	43,344.00
8	160.00	1,120.00	4,816.00	57,792.00
12	240.00	1,680.00	7,224.00	86,688.00

LEVEL III   32 DISPLAYS

Sales/Day (per display)	Profit/Day	Profit/Week	Profit/Month	Profit/Year
4	160.00	1,120.00	4,816.00	57,792.00
6	240.00	1,680.00	7,224.00	86,688.00
8	320.00	2,240.00	9,632.00	115,584.00
12	480.00	3,360.00	14,448.00	173,376.00

The above is a mathematical table and must not be construed as a guarantee of income or earnings. Each distributor's degree of success is directly attributed to the time and effort dedicated to the operation and expansion of his/her business

NOTE: The above computations are based on $1.25 profit per   sold.

(At fairs and special events   retails for $4.95 or a profit of $2.25.)

Sample 8

The projected profit page (see Sample #8) is the most important part of the pamphlet. All Americans shop at supermarkets and they are in tune to the volume of product that is being sold. The mooch also knows this but when he looks at the projected profit sheet, he is overwhelmed by the dollar figures. Just by selling 4 items a day in 8 locations he can make $1,204.00 a month. With 16 locations he can pocket almost $30,000.00 a year. IF THE LOCATIONS SELL 12 UNITS A DAY THE MOOCH WILL NET $86,688.00 A YEAR!! God has finally shown him a way to escape from his hum-drum existence and you the biz-op operator are his salvation.

PRICE LIST

LEVEL 1 FIRST TIME SET UP INCLUDES:

1. Distributorship for your area. Rights to market all   products. Rights to purchase all products wholesale.
2. Four floor model displays
3. Four counter displays
4. 864
5. Headers
6. Game instruction pamphlets
7. 288 Back-up

LEVEL 1 PACKAGE $6,000.00 PLUS U.P.S.

---

1. Distributorship for your area. Rights to market all   products. Rights to purchase all products wholesale.
2. Eight floor model displays.
3. Eight countertop displays
4. 1,724
5. Headers
6. Game instruction pamphlets
7. 576 Back-up

LEVEL 2 PACKAGE $11,500.00 PLUS U.P.S.

LEVEL 3 FIRST TIME SET UP INCLUDES:

1. Distributorship for your area. Rights to market all   products. Rights to purchase all products wholesale.
2. Sixteen floor model displays.
3. Sixteen countertop displays
4. 3,456
5. Headers
6. Game instruction pamphlets
7. 1,152 Back-up

LEVEL 3 PACKAGE $22,000.00 PLUS U.P.S.

At present the wholesale price on   is $1.75 each. The price fluctuates according to the price of rubber and shipping. The wholesale price of $1.75 each has stayed at this level for the last year.

Sample 9

The price list page (see Sample #9) should always have a nice spread. Some people can only make a minimum investment, others go crazy with greed and chunk out heavy duty bucks. Whatever they want to spend you take. The only thing you are looking at is closing as quickly as possible and collecting as much as you can.

Chapter 8: Best Products For A Novice

◆ ◆ ◆ ◆ ◆ ◆ ◆ ◆ ◆

Charity honor boxes are the bread and butter of the small biz-op operator. Honor boxes are also the best thing for a novice to try. They are easy to assemble and pitch. The charity box must be made of white cardboard. The ideal size for a charity honor box is 4 inches high, 24 inches deep, and 12 inches wide. Most Yellow Pages have listings for container companies. If the company does not have the exact box, they will have something similar.

I suggest you pick up two boxes to experiment with. You have to punch 10 neat rows of holes across the top. Each hole holds one Tootsie Pop. There should be a total of 100 Tootsie Pops stuck in the box's top. A slot that will accommodate a quarter needs to be cut in the top front of the box. A decal with the bold lettering "On Your Honor Please Deposit $.25" is to be glued right below the slot. Your charity's logo must be put on the box and be visible. (See sketch.) I usually use the National Federation of the Blind, but Chapter 6 lists several other charities.

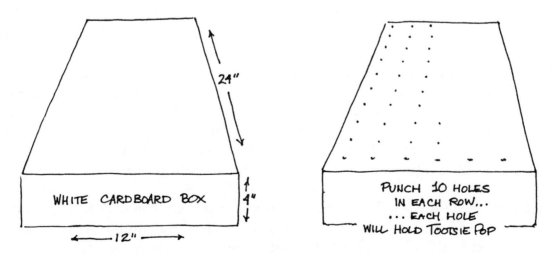

Assembly Instructions For Charity Honor Boxes (Page 1)

ON YOUR HONOR, PLEASE DEPOSIT
Charity Organization ▬ 25¢

Assembly Instructions For Charity Honor Boxes

One of the nice things about charity honor boxes is the start-up cost. The only out-of-pocket expense is the newspaper ad. This is a successful ad that I have used several times:

CHARITY HONOR BOXES
SUPER MONEY-MAKER

SMALL INVESTMENT — BIG RETURN
1-800-000-0000

Your basic phone pitch should be short and sweet. When you talk to the mooch, ask if he would like to make $125 a day without working. The answer is always an emphatic "yes." You can tell him you have customers throughout the country who are doing that on a daily basis with just 50 of your honor boxes. You explain that you have all the necessary charity connections and the only thing he has to do is collect the money, replace sold Tootsie Pops and pay the charity a small fee. You also explain that he will be the only one in his area handling your charity honor boxes (which is bullshit). You then ask if he would be interested in having a Fed-Ex package of information C.O.D. to him.

If he gives you any static about the C.O.D. charges, your comeback to him is, "We receive hundreds of requests daily. If we did not weed out the 'Lookie Lou's' we would go broke. So we only send pamphlets to people who are interested enough to pick up the C.O.D. charges." A true mooch will understand and give you the okay to overnight the package. (Fed-Ex charge – $10 to $15.) The idea is to get the package to the mooch as quickly as possible. The sooner the mooch gets the information, the faster you can close him.

You let the mooch have a day to digest the material. On the call-back you tell him there is another individual interested in the same area and that you deal on a first-come first-served basis. If he is first, he will have the entire area. He will also have the prime spots and be able to expand rapidly. Explain that his territory can profitably support 400 honor boxes and that translates into a daily net of $1,000. Assure the mooch that he will soon be able to become a full-time honor box route person. (One of the things I have learned about a mooch is that they all want to become independent and when you dangle that possibility in front of them it helps expedite the sale.) It is imperative that you work as quickly as possible. Never give a hot mooch time to cool off. You want to close him while he is still slobbering with greed.

Usually a mooch will want a day to go over all the data with his wife. This is when you give the mooch your singers' phone numbers and once again remind him there is another person interested in his area. You call the mooch 24 hours later and ask if he had a chance to talk to the references (your singers). (The singer, of course, has already told you what the mooch wanted to know.) If the singers have done their job you can usually close the deal by telling the mooch the other interested party will be calling back in the evening to either purchase the area or withdraw. But the mooch can alleviate the problem by overnighting a cashier's check for half the amount. (The other half will be collected when the honor boxes are delivered.)

Let the mooch know this is a great deal. He is getting started in a lucrative business at a fraction of what it would cost to open a cheap restaurant. He is only investing $2,500 in 50 honor boxes and another $1,000 in locating fees. (The locating fee is optional, but I've yet to run across a mooch who wanted to locate his own product.) For $3,500, he will be in a business that has the potential of netting $46,560 a year.

If the mooch gives you any argument, offer to go there in person and install the boxes, but he must send you half the money now and pay you the other half as soon as you arrive. "What we are looking for," you tell him, "are people who are willing to expand and become part of our family. The more you expand, the more boxes we sell. Unfortunately," you tell the "mooch," "I will have to charge you $20 per box to find premium locations, but I will give you a written guarantee that all the locations will be profitable." (See location guarantee in the Appendix.) "If after 90 days you have locations that are not generating the proper money, I will personally go back and relocate each one. Your success is my concern." (The 90-day guarantee gives the mooch plenty of time to become discouraged. Very few people abide by the contract and send in their weekly reports. In the end it makes no difference. The mooch is usually tired of the hassles and you should have changed your 1-800-number.)

This closing pitch, along with the enthusiasm of your singers and the projected profit sheet, should send the mooch to the nearest bank. That's good because you do not purchase any boxes until the mooch gives you the money.

As long as the mooch lives in a neighboring state, you can make the "going down there in person" promise, but if the mooch is on the other side of the country it is not profitable. You only want to make long trips when the mooch is kicking out 10 grand or more. The best way to back up a cross-country location guarantee is to hook the mooch up with a locating company. There is a list of U.S. Locating companies in the REFERENCE chapter.

Now to give you, the biz-op operator, an idea of how much you will make on an honor box job. If you run a 7-day newspaper ad in a city of 100,000 you should close three charity honor box deals. Here is the cost breakdown on 150 honor boxes.

Profits On Honor Box Project

♦ Cost of boxes – 150 @ $2.25 ea. = $337.50
♦ Two singers' fees (on honor boxes, the fee is $5 a unit) – $5 x 300 = $1,500. (Only to be paid if the deal closes.)
♦ Printing pamphlets (copies) – $.03 ea. X 100 sheets = $3.00
♦ Newspaper ad – It depends upon the paper, but I can safely round it off at $135.00 a week.
♦ 1-800 phone number (starter line incoming calls) – should not be over $50.00.
♦ Return calls on regular business phone – $175.00
♦ 15,000 Tootsie Pops – $450.00
♦ Two-day locating expenses (motel, food, gas) – $200.00
♦ Decals for honor boxes – $22.50
♦ Answering service – $45.00

Summary

Boxes	$ 337.50
Singers	1,500.00
Printing	3.00
Newspaper	135.00
1-800-number	50.00
Return calls	175.00
Tootsie Pops	450.00
Locating Expenses	200.00
Decals	22.50
Answering service	45.00
Total:	$2,918.00

Money Generated

Honor boxes — (Three packages, 50 units each) — $50 ea. x 150 = $7,500.00
Locating fee — $20 per unit x 150 = $3,000.00
Total: $10,500.00
Cost: 2,918.00
NET PROFIT: $7,582.00

(The honor box may also be used as a "how-to project." See Chapter 10.)

Raping The American Housewife
— Work-At-Home Programs

The American housewife is tailor-made for biz-op work-at-home programs. She is stuck at home — on a limited budget — with kids. Biz-op work-at-home programs offer her an opportunity to break out of her stagnated mold and become financially independent. For a few bucks, she has a fleeting chance to touch a deceptive dream of monetary freedom.

Every year millions of housewives respond to work-at-home ads. It is this vast pool of mooches that makes work-at-home programs easy pickings for the new, as well as the established, biz-opper.

One of the advantages to the work-at-home projects is cost. You do not need an answering service, phone number, 800 number or a suit. Your only start-up cost is a PO box, a false I.D. and advertising money.

There are six basic work-at-home business rules:

1. Run your ads in tabloids or housewife oriented romance magazines.
2. Do not run ads more than three times a year.
3. Do not run ads longer than three weeks.
4. Use a different PO box with each ad.
5. Use your false I.D. when renting a work-at-home PO box. (Work-at-home programs are on the government's possible mail fraud list. Because of this you want to keep a low profile.)
6. Only use a work-at-home project PO box for 60 days. You push your ad for three weeks, collect money for eight weeks, then close up shop.

My base work-at-home programs are "Stuffing Envelopes" and "Charity Boxes." You, as a biz-opper, can work with anything from assembling earrings to assembling Christmas ornaments.

Biz-oppers refer to work-at-home mooches as "bon-bon eaters." The average work-at-home mooch is a bon-bon eating, overweight, robe wearing, coffee-sucking housewife who wants to make an easy $1,000 a week. For a "starter kit" fee of $20 to $200 she expects you to show her the road to riches. Unfortunately her road dead ends in "Sucker Alley."

Work-at-home programs promise the mooch a net of $700 to $3,000 a week. Almost all are assembly oriented scams. The biz-opper makes money by selling the mooch a starter kit. The kits range from assembling electronic gadgets to Christmas ornaments. The mooch will pay from $20 to $200 for a biz-opper's starter kit.

"Turn your home into a small factory and become rich" is a phrase that has helped bag many a work-at-home mooch. That phrase, combined with a "money back guarantee" will cause a bon-bon eater to shake her piggy bank.

Guarantee, as I explain in Chapter 12, makes irresistible mooch bait. Anytime a mooch is convinced that her starter kit money is refundable, she will cut a hot trail to her local bank.

Before I go into my mooch work-at-home program, I will go over some of the work-at-home program "tags." The tags relate to the money back guarantees.

All of your assemble-at-home programs have inspection or time clauses. If you the biz-opper do not approve the work-at-home mooch's product, or if the product is not assembled within a certain time frame, you the biz-opper can reject it, thereby voiding the money back guarantee.

When I run a work-at-home biz-op program, it's only for 60 days. If the mooch decides within 30 days that she doesn't want to assemble the product and she requests her money back, I just ignore her. Basically, the guarantee you are giving the bon-bon eater doesn't mean shit. If they send you finished products, you reject them. If they want their money back, you ignore them. Rake in as much as you can, then disappear. Work-at-home projects are always good for at least $2,000 a week. The best time to run your work-at-home ads are September, October and November. The bon-bon eaters look at work-at-home programs as a way to create extra Christmas money. In reality, it's the biz-opper who ends up with the Christmas bonus.

When running ads for work-at-home mooches, I use the tabloids. The tabloids seem to have a surplus of bon-bon eaters. The *National Enquirer* has a circulation of 18 million. The same people also control the *Star*. Rates in the *National Enquirer* are $8.95 a word with a 10-word minimum. The *Star* is $7.20 a word with a 10-word minimum. The *Enquirer* and the *Star* will sometimes ask for a copy of the letter you will be sending the mooch. As long as you use a variation of my formatted mooch bait letter, you will not have any trouble. The *National Enquirer* and the *Star* can be contacted at (800) 223-6226; address: PO Box 10178, Clearwater, FL 34617. The Globe tabloid group consists of the *Globe*, the *National Examiner* and the *Sun*; combined circulation, 3 million. Your ad automatically is run in all three tabloids. Cost, $6.10 per word with a 10-word minimum. The Globe tabloid group doesn't care what you send in or who you screw. Just send them a cashier's check along with your ad and, bingo, you're in business — my kind of people. Address: Globe Tabloid Classified Group, PO Box 21, Rouses Point, NY 12979-0021, phone (514) 849-7733.

As you can see, one of the advantages to the tabloids is circulation. If you run the right ad at the right time of the year (just before Christmas) you can expect an overwhelming response. If just one-half of one percent of a million people sent you a S.A.S.E., you would have 5,000 bon-bon eaters on line. If only 500 of those responded at $20 each, you would gross 10 grand.

Work-At-Home Ads

Here are some typical work-at-home ads:

```
ASSEMBLE OUR devices at home. We pay up to $1,000 weekly.
No experience. Send SASE to BIG TIME MONEY, Suite 44,
L.A., CA 88877.
```
(The cost of this ad for one week in the *Globe* is $134.20.)

HOME MILLIONAIRES INC., 400 Dollar Way, Suite 3, El Paso, TX 67754.
(Cost to run this ad for one week in the *Globe*, $158.60.)

MAKE HOLIDAY earrings at home! We pay up to $1,000 weekly. Year-round opportunity. No experience. Rush stamped envelope to BIG BUCKS, 62 Diamond Crest, Suite 9, NY, NY 66654.
(Cost in the *Globe*, $152.50.)

Work-At-Home Mooch Bait Letter

The following is a sample of a work-at-home mooch bait letter a biz-opper sends to a bon-bon eater.

MAKE BEAUTIFUL HAND-ASSEMBLED
GLASS-BEADED EARRINGS AT HOME

Hello there! Thank you for your interest in this excellent opportunity! Now you can make $60,000 to $100,000 a year in the comfort of your own home by making simple, beautiful glass-beaded earrings. No experience is necessary, we show both men and women assemblers how to make our fine products.

Big Bucks Earrings are some of the loveliest and most unique on the market today. We currently need independent contractors who would like to make $100,000 a year. We are looking for contractors who will take pride in assembling a top-of-the-line product.

UP TO $2,000 A WEEK!!!

We will pay you $500 for every 50 sets of earrings you produce according to our specifications. If you can assemble 200 earrings a week, WE WILL PAY YOU $2,000.

HERE'S THE PLAN

Big Bucks Earring Company will provide you with a starter kit, which will give you everything you need to start producing earrings for profit. These packages represent a remarkable money-making opportunity. Your starter kit contains enough beads and charms, thread, beading, needles, earring hooks and threaders to make 10 individual earrings. Your starter kit also includes clear instructions, illustrations and a photo of the finished product, so you can get to work making your first earrings.

CHOOSE THE EARRING OF YOUR CHOICE

With Big Bucks Earring Company, you have the opportunity to choose the earring with colors that appeal to you. (After we have purchased 50 earring sets from you, we reserve the right to send you a new design. We always need to vary our inventory.) We now have two strikingly beautiful designs you can choose from.

HERE ARE THE DESIGNS WE CURRENTLY NEED

Far East Symphony — A dramatic piece of jewelry. Dark blue beads combine with gold for a mysterious, ancient look. Set with glowing amber and green glass beads.

Victorian Fantasy — A feminine, tinkling vision with lavender, pink and blue glass beads, featuring golden hearts and roses.

Both designs are elegant and creative, yet they are actually derived from simple, traditional beading patterns found in many craft magazines. Thousands all over America have used these techniques for decades. Big Bucks Earrings uses these age-old methods, then enhances the traditional design with inventive and creative new use of colors and textures.

Big Buck Home-Based Supplier Agreement

Please Print Clearly or Type

Name _____

Address _____

City _____ **State** _____ **Zip** _____

Social Security # _____ **Phone (____)** _____

Big Buck Earring Company will pay $500 for every unit of 50 pairs of earrings you send us made to our specifications, up to $2,000 per week maximum. Big Buck will send you a Supplier Starter Kit, with copyrighted instructions, patterns and diagrams necessary to make the earring design you choose. You will also get a Quality Checklist which will clearly explain our standards so you can check your earrings before sending them in. Also included will be materials and supplies for your first 10 earrings, and instructions for obtaining more supplies. Unfortunately, even with the best intentions not everyone follows through with the work. Since it costs us time and money to register a new Home-Based Supplier and send a kit, we must require a REFUNDABLE registration fee of $35.

Registration entitles you to:

➤Rights to use Big Buck's copyrighted designs for the earring you choose.

➤Our promise to purchase up to 200 pairs of earrings per week made to our specifications

➤Unlimited rights to sell Big Buck earrings to others at a price of your choice

➤Entry into our computerized Supplier Payment System

➤Optional inspection of your first earrings, with tips and suggestions when needed

➤And of course, a complete Starter Kit as described above

Big Buck cannot pay for partially-completed work or incomplete units. Naturally, since we must sell what we buy from you, we must insist that all earrings meet the quality standards clearly defined in the Quality Checklist supplied with your starter kit. We reserve the right to refuse your first unit, for which you have 60 days. Since this is more than enought time to complete a unit, we cannot extend these deadlines for any reason. When you want to quit, just don't send any units for 30 days and you will be replaced without obligation. As a Home-Based Supplier you are a self-employed independent contractor, so we deduct no taxes and you are responsible for your own tax records.

NO-RISK REFUND POLICY protects you TWO ways!
First, if for any reason you decide not to participate, you may return your starter kit in the same condidtion you received it within 15 days of our shipping date (stamped on the outside of your kit) for full refund of the $35 registration fee, no questions asked. Second, after you have become a steady Big Buck supplier, your registration fee of $35 will be REFUNDED IN FULL with our purchase of your tenth unit.

I HAVE READ AND UNDERSTAND THE TERMS OF THIS AGREEMENT.

Please register me as a Big Buck Home-Based Supplier and send me my Starter Kit.

Signature _____ Date _____

I Have Enclosed: ❑ Money Order (allow 2-3 weeks for shipping except for RUSH shipping)   ❑ Check (allow 5 to 6 weeks for shipping and check clearing)

I would like to make the following design:
(NOTE: Please choose carefully, no kit exchanges)   *Please fill in completely:*

Registration Fee: Victorian Fantasy, $35 .... ❑$ _____ (refundable)

Far East Symphony, $35 .... ❑ $ _____ (refundable)

Shipping and Handling .... $ ____6.95.. (non-refundable)

RUSH SHIPPING (money orders only, non-refundable), $2   ❑ $ _____ (optional)

Total enclosed $ _____ .

PLEASE sign and photocopy this agreement for your records,

then mail this ENTIRE PAGE with payment to: **Big Buck**
Suite 44, Los Angeles, CA 88877

MAKE CHECKS OR MONEY ORDERS PAYABLE TO BIG BUCK.
Sorry, offer not good in Canada.. This offer is void where prohibited.   © 1993 Big Buck Co.

Work-At-Home Earring Project Application Form

Cost Of Earring Work-At-Home Starter Kit

Each starter kit contains enough product to assemble 10 sets of earrings.

20 pieces of string	.02
20 earring hooks (.05 ea.)	$2.00
20 eye pins (.05 ea.)	$1.00
200 plastic beads, assorted colors	.60
20 glass beads, assorted colors	.20
Instructions (copy)	.03
Small, cheap shipping box	.25
(Bon-bon eater pays postage.)	
Total Cost, One Kit:	4.10
Cost of a starter kit to mooch:	35.00
(plus postage)	
Biz-op cost:	4.10
	_____
Net:	$30.90

When you advertise in the tabloids for three weeks you should mail out at least 200 kits.

Cost on 200 starter kits	820.00
Advertising	450.00
PO Box	38.00
	_____
TOTAL	1,308.00
200 starter kits cost to mooches	7,000.00
(plus postage)	
Cost to biz-opper	1,308.00
	_____
PROFIT:	$5,692.00

Putting together a work-at-home program is not hard. Be creative. Figure your costs. Find a product that sounds easy to assemble, but also satisfies the mooch's greed factor. Biz-oppers who create the most appealing products are the ones who really cash in.

BIG BUCK *Easy* EARRING

Materials

a. 6"-9" cord
b. 20 plastic "seed" beads
c. 1 large glass bead
d. 1 earring wire

Assembly Instructions

① String plastic beads onto cord.

② Put both ends of cord thru glass bead.

③ Thread ends thru loop in earring wire.

④ Bring ends back thru glass bead (can use needle to push cord).

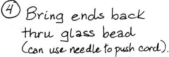

⑤ Tie knot, trim & tuck ends into bottom of glass bead.

Finished Product

Work-At-Home Earring Assembly Instructions

Stuffing Envelopes

The stuffing envelopes project is the easiest of the tabloid biz-op scams. I'm always amazed that people seriously believe that they can make $1,000 a week stuffing envelopes. Evidently, greed and the "something for nothing" ploy are too much for the bon-bon eater to resist. What the mooch doesn't know is stuffing envelopes is a sophisticated, highly mechanized operation that is run by legitimate businesses that specialize in mass mailings. The possibility of them using a bon-bon eater is not only remote, it's a joke. As a biz-opper, you look upon bon-bon eaters as a joke — a profitable joke.

I have been running my stuffing envelopes ads for eight years. Once a year I will run a three week tabloid ad similar to these:

> EARN $1,000 a week processing mail. Guaranteed. Start immediately. Free details. Send self-addressed, stamped envelope to WW Marketing, Suite 99, NY, NY 99866.
>
> (Cost in the *Globe* for one week: $122.00.)

> EARN $3,000 per 1,000 envelopes stuffed. Send self-addressed, stamped envelope to VS, Dept. 10, 731 Woodburn Ave., Phoenix, AZ 66789.
>
> (One week in the *Globe*: $91.50.)

> Make $2,000 WEEKLY stuffing envelopes. Send SASE to Christian Distributing, Suite 22, Lynn Haven, TX 93224.
>
> (*Globe* cost, one week: $91.50.)

When I receive a bon-bon's SASE, I send the following mooch bait letter (See pages 49 and 50). Note that there is no phone number on the letter, only a suite number.

Big Stuffers, Inc.

Suite 66, Golden, Co. 22435

Make $1,000 Weekly

Stuffing Envelopes

Dear Friend:

CAN YOU STUFF AND MAIL 1,000 ENVELOPES EACH WEEK FOR $1,000.00? **If your answer is YES! then our company needs you. We are seeking folks who want to improve their standard of living ... Folks who want more money ... more job satisfaction ... more security ... and more of al the good things in life. We have every reason to believe that we are looking for someone like YOU.**

Your job will be to **SECURE, STUFF and MAIL ENVELOPES FOR OUR COMPANY.** You will be paid at the rate of **$1.00 for each envelope that you stuff with our business circulars.** If you stuff 500 envelopes, you will be paid $500.00 ... if you stuff 1,000 envelopes, you will be paid $1,000, and so on. **You will be paid for every single envelope that you secure and stuff with our business circulars ... at the rate of $1.00 for each envelope.** Your payment for the envelopes you stuff and send to us is **GUARANTEED!** You Will Be Paid Promptly! No Long Wait For Checks To Arrive! You will receive $1.00 for each envelope on a regular basis. Stuff as many envelopes as you receive and you will be paid for every single one. When you receive our instructions, you will see that we mean everything that we say in this letter. We will show you how to **STUFF OUR ENVELOPES and MAKE MORE MONEY DAY AFTER DAY, and WEEK AFTER WEEK** for as long as you want. Of course you are not obligated to us ... and you can choose your own working hours ... start working when you want and stop when you want. You can quit our program anytime and even re-join at a later date if you wish. We try to make things as easy as possible for **YOU.**
We need your help badly ... because we have more work than our local staff can handle. We would like to mail our offers to thousands of people in the U.S.A. and Canada. If we give out our stuffing and mailing jobs to homeworkers like you, we save a lot of money that we would normally have to spend to get more office space and more office workers. We can afford to pay $1,000 for stuffing 1,000 envelopes and will save money that normally would be spent on overhead and office expenses.

Our System Of Stuffing Envelopes is very simple ... You will not have to buy any envelopes or postage stamps. We supply all circulars free of charge. By following our instructions you will receive all the envelopes to be stuffed. All envelopes are already addressed and have the postage stamps pasted on. **No licking stamps or addressing envelopes!**

Anyone can do this kind of work! The only requirement is that you must be 18 years or older. Place of residence does not matter! ... You can live in a large city or a small village. Education does not matter! As long as you can read and write simple English, you qualify to stuff envelopes for our company. ......**IMAGINE STUFFING 500 ENVELOPES AND COLLECTING $500... OR STUFFING 1,000 ENVELOPES AND COLLECTING $1,000.** Our company can make it happen for you ... just like we make it happen for other folks just like **YOU.** Please note that this is not a chain letter of a pyramid scheme ... You will not be asked to

Envelope Stuffing Mooch Bait Letter (Page 1)

stuff anything objectionable … You will not have to sign any contracts … **AND BEST OF ALL, YOU WILL NOT HAVE TO BUY ANYTHING ELSE FROM US IN ORDER TO GET STARTED …** and there is no other work involved except what we say.

In order to eliminate those folks who are not serious about earning money by stuffing envelopes, but are just out to satisfy their curiosity, we have decided to ask each participant for a $35.00 registration fee. THIS $35.00 DEPOSIT IS FULLY REFUNDABLE. As soon as you send us your first 200 stuffed envelopes we will return your deposit plus the cost for mailing the envelopes to us.

This opportunity to secure and stuff envelopes for our company is **LIMITED**. This means that as soon as we get enough folks to register we will stop taking applications. So don't let this **ONE TIME EXTRA INCOME OPPORTUNITY** pass you by. We urge you to consider this opportunity while you still have time. Think of your future and let us hear from you TODAY!!

MONEY BACK GUARANTEE!! We guarantee that as soon as you send us your first 200 envelopes that you have secured and stuffed with our circulars, you will receive $200.00 payment plus **A REFUND OF YOUR $35.00 REGISTRATION FEE**. We will also pay you for the cost of mailing the envelopes to us…This way the instructions and starting supplies cost you nothing. Send us as many envelopes as you want … work as long as you want … Stop and re-join our program anytime you want without paying any extra fee. This is our complete guarantee to you.

To Start earning money quickly … just fill out and rush the registration form to us. As soon as we get it we will rush your instructions and starting supplies to you. **Don't delay! Act Today!** The sooner we hear from you the sooner you can **START**.

Sincerely yours,

Big Stuffers, Inc.

REGISTRATION FORM

❑ Check   ❑ Cash   ❑ Money Order
❑ Enclosed is $35.00. Please rush my starting supplies and instructions.
❑ I am sending $2.00 extra. PLEASE RUSH my supplies by FIRST CLASS MAIL

SEND ORDERS TO: BIG STUFFERS, INC., SUITE 66, GOLDEN, CO 22435.

Name _____

Address _____

City _____ State _____ Zip _____

Amount of money you want to make weekly ❑ $500.00 ❑ $1,000.00 ❑ MORE

Please Note: Registration fee paid by cash or money order will be processed and supplies shipped in 5 days. Checks are held for clearance.

Envelope Stuffing Mooch Bait Letter (Page 2)

Once you receive the bon-bon mooch's money you send this letter:

> Dear (Bon-Bon):
>
> Congratulations on your decision to become an envelope stuffer. With this letter, you now have the tool to make, as I do, $1,000 a week. In order to make money stuffing envelopes, all that's required is for you to run the following ad in a tabloid or local newspaper:
>
> MAKE $1,000 WEEKLY stuffing envelopes. Send stamped, self-addressed envelope to (insert the name of your company here).
>
> After you have run your ad, all you do is wait for people to send you their SASEs. (Just like I waited for you to send me your SASE.) When you receive the $35, you simply send them a copy of the letter you are now holding. You should easily receive 50 letters a week, giving you a net of $1,000 weekly.
>
> **GOOD LUCK ON YOUR NEW**
> **ENVELOPE STUFFING VENTURE**
>
> THANKS,
> BIG STUFFERS, INC.

What is really nice about bon-bon eaters is they are always short on cash. In other words, they do not have the capital to run a national ad. They also believe they have been taken and if they do the same thing to someone else they might be arrested. There is a question of mail fraud involved with all the tabloid programs. But as long as you use a different mail box for each project and use your false I.D., you will remain undetected.

Cost Of Envelope Stuffing Project

The cost includes sending out 5,000 mooch letters and selling 500 envelope stuffer starter kits.

Three weeks of advertising in tabloids	450.00
PO Box	38.00
5,000 copies of mooch bait letter	50.00
(@ $.03 ea.)	
500 copies of final envelope stuffing letter	15.00
(@ $.03 ea.)	
500 envelopes	20.00
Postage, 500 stamps	145.00
Total:	718.00
Cost to mooches on 500 kits	17,500.00
(@ $35 ea.)	
PROFIT:	$ 16,782.00

Charity Work-At-Home Program

The only difference between the work-at-home mooch and the vending machine mooch is money. The work-at-home housewife is usually limited to a $20 to $200 investment, while the vending mooch is always good for several grand. Both seem to be drawn toward what they think is easy charity money. My successful work-at-home charity ad reads:

```
NEW! HOT! Work at home. Make $1,000 weekly assembling
charity products. Send SASE to Charity Marketing, Suite
2020, Chicago, IL 99984.
```
(Cost in the *Globe* for one week: $128.20.)

When I receive the mooch's SASE, I send this mooch bait letter:

Hello,

Thank you for inquiring into America's newest and hottest work-at-home program. Our program is the least time consuming and most profitable on the market. It can make you up to $8,000 a month (depending on how many boxes you assemble), while contributing to a needy charity.

We at Charity Marketing are privileged to work with and help three nationally recognized charities. These charities all depend upon programs like ours and on people like you. Not only will you be helping them, but you will also be financially helping yourself.

There is nothing complicated or expensive about our program. All you have to do is assemble the boxes and place them in designated locations. You then collect the money weekly, send the charity $2.00 per box per month and keep the rest for yourself.

Why is a charity willing to accept $2.00 and let you keep the rest? In a time of recession, charities are more than happy to accept a smaller amount. At the present time, most charities are struggling just to keep their programs afloat. Remember you are doing all the work. Even though it is easy and fun, you still have to assemble boxes, collect money and keep books. You are the middle person. Without people like you, the charities would lose millions.

The amount of money you make depends upon the number of boxes you assemble. Using our simple, copyrighted method, you can quickly put together 50 charity boxes. You then place them in the stores on our list and begin collecting money. You will have a legal contract with the charity you are collecting for. WITH 50 CHARITY HONOR BOXES YOU CAN MAKE UP TO $1,000 A WEEK!!! All that's required is the initial labor in assembling your boxes and a few hours a week collecting money.

This is the biggest money maker and easiest work-at-home program on the market today.

For $99.95 plus postage your charity honor box work-at-home starter kit will include:

1. Copyrighted assembly instructions.

2. 10 unassembled, sturdy, beautiful pink boxes (We make our money selling you more boxes at $9.95 each.)

3. Legal charity contract that you sign and send in to the participating charity.

4. List of local businesses to put the charity boxes into.

5. Our IRON CLAD GUARANTEE. If within 30 days you change your mind, just return your boxes unassembled and we will promptly return all your money.

THERE IS NO WAY YOU CAN LOSE. Just fill out the enclosed paper work, attach a cashier's check and you will be in business.

THANK YOU,
CHARITY MARKETING

Biz-Opper Cost On Charity Marketing Starter Kit

10 boxes.(Purchase pie boxes at local bakery) (@ $.15 ea.)	$1.50
Copies of charities' agreements (See the Appendix.)	.09
Assembly instructions copy (See next page.)	.03
Location list copy (See Chapter 7.)	.03
Large padded envelopes, 20"x14" (mooch pays postage)	1.75
Total:	3.40
Cost of Starter Kit to Mooch:	99.95
Cost of Starter Kit to Biz-Opper:	3.40
PROFIT:	$96.55

If you run your tabloid ad for three weeks you should sell at least 100 charity starter kits.

Tabloid advertising cost	$ 450.00
Cost of 100 starter kits to biz-opper	340.00
PO Box	39.00
Total:	829.00
Cost of 100 Starter Kits to Mooches	9,995.00
Cost of Starter Kits to Biz-opper	829.00
PROFIT:	$9,166.00

Chapter 9:
Jackpots

◆ ◆ ◆ ◆ ◆ ◆ ◆ ◆ ◆

Another high-profit, easy to assemble project for the beginner is the Jackpot. The Jackpot's clear acrylic pipe is 28 inches in length, $\frac{1}{8}$-inch thick, and has an inside diameter of 4 inches. The acrylic pipe costs between $5 and $7 a foot. The boot, or bottom, is a piece of colored plastic 8 inches x 8 inches and ½-inch thick. A $\frac{1}{8}$-inch thick, 5-inch long acrylic rod is glued to the center of the plastic bottom. On the top of the acrylic rod is glued a 1 inch x 1 inch x ½-inch thick plastic coin catcher. A hot glue gun is used to attach the boot to the acrylic pipe. (See diagram.) Total cost, including glue, $19.95.

The Jackpot is still new and a good product to hit the classifieds with. (The Jackpot may also be used as a "How-To Project," see Chapter 10.) It's a game people play for charity. The object of the game is to try and drop a quarter on the plastic coin catcher.

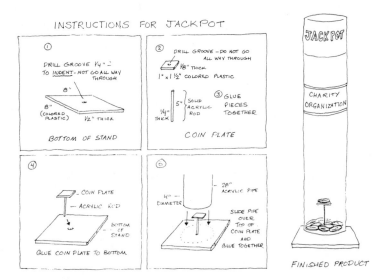

Assembly Instructions For Jackpot

You locate Jackpots by using charities. I did mine using the National Federation of the Blind. The pitch is, "It's a fund-raiser and would only be in for 30 days. We did this across country last year and it generated almost $500,000." (See Chapter 6 for entire pitch.) With this pitch you can easily place 25 units a day.

Jackpot Newspaper Ads

```
NEW FOR THE '90s. Best solid business opportunity in
America today. No selling. Charity related. All cash
business. You need $4,000 to $10,000 for equipment. CALL -

ALL CASH BIZ. Qualified individuals needed with ability to
handle large amounts of cash. No selling. Ideal part time.
Charity. 4K-10K investment. Areas going fast. Call

NEW GAME MACHINE. Just collect cash. No selling. Charity
$$ maker of the '90s. Must have 4K for equipment. Areas
going fast. Call
```

Your intro phone pitch is:

Have you seen charity honor boxes? (Yes.) *Well, our charity fun machine is more popular and makes more money without the hassle of stocking or carrying candy products. Right now we have distributors who are making $1,000 a week off 50 machines. Our biggest distributors have 200 fun machines and they are netting almost $4,000 a week.*

We are looking for an exclusive distributor in your area. If you are that person, we will guarantee that you will make money because we will be able to cream the area getting you the best locations. Just like the first candy machines, you will be getting in on the ground floor of a new deal. The only thing we want is for you to expand. Does this sound like something you might be interested in? (Yes, but what kind of machine is it?) *It's a new fun device that allows a quarter to be inserted into it.*

(Don't give them a lot of info about the Jackpot. Make them take the Fed-Ex package.) *In order to get you all the pertinent information, we need to Fed-Ex a C.O.D. package of material.*

If you have him "hooked," he'll give you the O.K. If not, go on to the next call. (You will get a lot of calls on a $4,000 biz-op ad, especially when it relates to a charity.)

Mooch Bait Letter

Dear

We at S.S. Corporation want to thank you for your interest in the ALL NEW JACKPOT FUN MACHINE.

We have spent months and many, many dollars on research, development, and test marketing this exciting machine. After you have read this booklet, we are sure that you will feel the same as we do — THIS IS A WINNER!!!!!! We have "THE SENSATION" of the '90s.

We are certain you will agree this is the best business opportunity in America today. For as little as $4,000, you can start your own business. You need no office or warehouse space, no advertising budget or utility bills. Best of all, there is no product to sell. You only collect the money from the Jackpot every week and count it. You are only obligated to send the sponsoring charity $2 a month. Locations — Every business is a prospect. They are all willing to donate the space to the charity. Anyone can easily place 50 Jackpots in one day. (*Bullshit. I've yet to see a mooch place one.*) If you do not want to place the Jackpots, we have professional locators with years of experience who will secure premium spots. Of course, there is a fee.

Either way — if you place your Jackpots or have them professionally located — we are sure this is the best opportunity available today. You will have a five-year contract with the charity. Take a day to read over the enclosed material. We will call back with information on distributors who have become financially independent.

Profit On Jackpot Project

Cost Of Jackpot Project
(20 unit deal)

Material (includes glue)	$ 399.00
$19.95/unit x 20	
Boxes — need 5 boxes x $10	50.00
(4 Jackpots per box)	
Copies of marketing pamphlet:	30.00
Singers — $20/unit x 20	400.00
(paid only if the deal closes)	
1-800-number (above average response):	65.00
Return calls (above average):	150.00
Answering service:	75.00
Locating expense:	250.00
	————
Total Costs:	$1,419.00

- Jackpots have sold for as high as $200 and as low as $100. For this example, we will price them at $150. Twenty Jackpots x $150 = $3,000.
- Locating - $150/unit x 20 = $3,000.

Summary:

Jackpots	$3,000.00
Locating	3,000.00
Total:	$6,000.00
Cost of Product:	1,419.00
Profit:	$4,581.00

Chapter 10:
Voice Mail

◆ ◆ ◆ ◆ ◆ ◆ ◆ ◆ ◆

Voice mail is a good tool for beginners as well as pros. This type of biz-op marketing is used mainly to sell $35 to $100 how-to packages (how to get-rich-overnight plans).

Voice mail is like an answering machine, but instead of just taking messages, it sells your product. Voice mail boxes are inexpensive. Rentals run about $15 a month. Many private mail box rental places have voice mail boxes. For larger projects (10-25 boxes), you switch to your phone company. When you rent a voice mail box, you have complete control over what you want to record.

These are the major steps in a voice mail project:

◆ Get voice mail box - $15/month.
◆ Have 1-800-number transferred to voice mail (optional).
◆ Record mail box pitch (one to two minutes).
◆ Run newspaper ads.
◆ When you receive mooch's $4 check, send him the info letter.
◆ Mooch responds to info letter by sending you $35 check for complete package.

You can utilize your 1-800-number for voice mail by contacting your 1-800 carrier and telling them you want to transfer your 1-800-number from your answering service to a voice mail box. AT&T calls their service the "800 call waiting" system. It only costs $20 for the transfer. If you do not use AT&T's "800 call waiting" system, there is a $30 charge to piggyback the line to the voice mail box. Then there is another $30 charge to have it re-hooked to your answering service. If you use AT&T's 1-800-number call waiting, you can transfer your 1-800-number back to your answering service by using a special code. There is no charge for this. AT&T can also fill your voice mail box needs. I suggest you stay with the voice mail box's phone number to start with. No need running up a 1-800-number bill.

Two projects that I had a lot of success with were "Assembling Your Own Honor Boxes" and "The Jackpot Fun Machine." I sold the how-to booklets for $35. I eventually hit a gross of $5,000 a week. In order to do this type of volume, you must do two things. Have at least 10 voice mail boxes and have something that catches the public's eye. Charity vending is an eye catcher. I gave the public a chance to get into the high-priced field of charity vending for a song.

Here are some tips on voice mail box sales. Place your ad in three different daily newspapers. You do not want to make a massive newspaper jump until you know if you have a winner. Give the ads a month, and if at that time you're filling 75 to 100 orders a week, go big time.

This is my successful "Assembling Your Own Honor Box" program. It begins with these ads:

```
$500 WK. POSSIBLE. Work with new charity vend system. Own
your own business. Very little cash needed. 1-800-000-
Ext.-5
```

```
ECONOMICAL CHARITY VENDS. Why spend $5K-$10K on charity
honor boxes? My new charity system delivers 50 boxes for
under $150. Call 800-Ext 10.
```

This is the recorded voice mail box pitch the mooch hears:

Thank you for calling. If you are calling about the ad, you must be interested in charity vending. Most big marketing companies that deal in charity vending are rip-offs. They charge from $50 to $75 for small charity vends and up to $800 for larger vending machines. Our company, Charity Marketing, is making it possible for a person to get into this business without hocking their house. We have developed a system where you, the entrepreneur, will only pay $2.50 for a charity vend — a charity vend that will make just as much as a $100 vend. We also have a collection of testimonials from large U.S. firms that have taken and will take charity vends. Fifty $2.50 vends can bring in $500 a week.

All of our charities are registered with the federal government.

If you would like more information, just send a check for $4 to: Charity Marketing, 1733 H Street, Suite 757, Chicago, Illinois 98230 and I will send it out to you right away.

For $4 the mooch gets the following letter.

"Assembling Your Own Honor Box"
Pitch Letter

Dear Customer:

Thanks for your interest in my company.

After working for 10 years with different charity marketing companies, I became convinced that the customer, the person buying the charity marketing products (vending machines, honor boxes), was being taken. I know that charity vending is good for the charities, but it was not good for people buying the charity honor boxes. I have watched the vending marketing companies charge people $800 for a $100 vending machine and $75 for a $5 honor box. People who wanted to get into business were selling their kids for these overpriced vends. It was unfair and I decided to develop a system that would allow the first time entrepreneur to get his toes wet for under $150.

Using my system, your honor boxes only cost $2.50. Why are they so reasonable? Because you assemble them.

In September of 1990 I formed a company that not only helped the charities, but also gave the buyer an even break. Instead of going into debt to purchase charity vending machines and honor boxes, a person can now utilize my method and make the same amount at a fraction of the cost.

The packet you receive from my company will have legal charity contracts from four different charities. It will also have information about the charities. All you have to do is choose the charity you want to work with. Each month you send the charity $1.50 to $2.50 (depending on which charity you choose). That means it will only take one display a week and a half to make the money for the charity. The remaining money generated over 30 days will go into your pocket.

Example: One vend can generate $10 a week; 50 vends generate $500 a week. That translates into a monthly gross of $2,000. Out of that $2,000 you pay the charity $75, leaving you with a net of $1,925. All charities are aware of this, but in this time of recession, they are happy to receive any money.

Our package will take you a step at a time through the assembly of the charity vends. There are several different displays you can choose from. Some displays hold products, others do not. You will not believe how easy they are to assemble. Why spend $3,000 to $10,000 when you can purchase our packet for $35 and assemble 50 charity displays yourself for under $150?! A $2.50 vend will make just as much as a $100 vend. I GUARANTEE IT.

YOUR CHARITY MARKETING PACKAGE WILL INCLUDE:

1. Instructions and diagrams on where to get and how to assemble $2.50 honor boxes. Everything will be diagrammed. They are easy and fun to do. Especially when they start bringing the money in.

2. Instructions and diagrams on how to assemble Jackpots, the hottest and highest grossing charity vend in the country today. Putting together Jackpots is a snap. There are only four pieces to assemble. We have signed statements from major restaurants verifying that the Jackpots have taken in as much as $1,348 in 45 days. The Jackpot is a non-product vend. In other words, it has no candy in it. People put their money in Jackpots because they enjoy playing it and at the same time they are contributing a portion of it to a charity.

3. You will receive four charity contracts. You have the option of picking out the charity you want. When you have filled out and sent in the contract, you will become a legal representative of that charity. Many of these charities depend upon operators like you to help cover their overhead. Some of our charities collect as much as $500,000 a year from charity vending operators. That means the money you send in is making a big difference.

The charities' monthly fees vary from $1.50 to $2.50 per charity vending unit. Also in this package will be information on the charities and charity locating forms.

4. You will receive testimonials from national businesses (including a variety of restaurant chains) in reference to the charity vends. These testimonials will allow you to place your vends in these and other premium locations. Just by showing these testimonials, companies (many chain fast food restaurants) will be more than happy to accept the charity vends. If you are thinking of getting into this business, but do not want to be ripped off for overpriced vends, Charity Marketing has the answer. Why pay $5,000 to $10,000 for honor boxes and vending machines when, for a small investment of $35, I can show you how to put out 50 honor boxes for under $150? These $2.50 honor boxes will make you more than the larger, expensive vends because you will have more of them.

Just compare 50 of the $2.50 vends to 50 of the $75 vends. You are looking at a savings of $3,600. Ask the big charity marketing companies if they have testimonials you can use to place their vends. They won't know what you are talking about. The only thing they want is to squeeze you for every dime you have. Don't let the big vending companies get fat off your money.

**WITH OUR SYSTEM, *YOU* WILL MAKE THE MONEY,
NOT THE BIG MARKETING COMPANY.**

Send your check for $35 to Charity Marketing, 1733 H Street, Suite 757, Chicago, IL 98230.

I WANT YOU TO SUCCEED.

THANK YOU,

CHARITY MARKETING

When you receive the $35.00 check, you send out a package that includes: the sketch of the Jackpot, the sketch of the honor box, the list of places that have the plastic parts for the Jackpot, the list of places that have the boxes for the honor boxes, the contracts from four different charities, and the locating agreements from the four different charities. (See the REFERENCE Chapter and the Appendix.)

Chapter 11: Hook

◆ ◆ ◆ ◆ ◆ ◆ ◆ ◆ ◆

Your initial contact with the mooch will be via the telephone. Phone pitching is the first step in setting the "hook." Once you have the mooch committed to accepting your C.O.D. marketing package, you have started the "money reach."

THE PRODUCTS YOU SELL NEED BRAND NAME FAMILIARITY. In other words, you need to draw a correlation between your product and a brand name product. When I was working with Spacebal (a toy ball with a latex loop running through it), I pitched it as the Frisbee Hoola-Hoop of the '90s. If it was a skin lotion, I used Max Factor. The old reliable for a gas or oil additive is STP. With plant products or seeds it was Lilly. Always stay with a product that allows you to use a brand name similarity. It makes your phone pitch much easier when you paint the mooch a recognizable picture. Another important part of the phone pitch is the "Big figure gross." The larger the gross of the industry your product is attached to, the better it sounds. Sports and toys gross over $60 billion a year, cosmetics $40 billion, automotive products $70 billion, and vending $10 billion. Give the mooch figures so dazzling he will automatically assume he can get a tiny piece of the pie.

Always promise the mooch an exclusive distributorship. Use Coke and McDonald's as examples. Tell him 50 years ago a Coke distributorship sold for $750. Now the same distributorship is worth millions. Remind him that McDonald's started back in the '50s and at that time a franchise cost only $8,000. Now the franchise fee is $1 million.

You cannot guarantee this product will become as successful, but let him know the product is selling well in different parts of the country and he is getting in on a ground floor opportunity. If the product makes it big, so will he.

The following is an example of how I found a product and put a marketing and pitch program together. Spacebal was a toy product that I ran across in a small Washington town. It was a weird, well-constructed toy. A thick, hollow latex loop ran out of a solid 2-inch rubber ball. The idea was to place the loop on the end of your thumb, pull back, and fire the ball into the air. Wham. It would take off about 200 feet. If the thing were to hit you at close range, it would be an ass knocker. Spacebal reminded me somewhat of a slingshot with a ball attached to it. It looked more like a weapon than a toy.

I discovered it at a small street fair. After talking to the man in the booth, I found out it was being produced locally. Unfortunately, sales were non-existent and they had stopped production. He was just trying to sell off some of the inventory, but wasn't having much luck. I instantly saw the possibility of biz-opping the product. When I found out there were 50,000 of them in storage, I was overcome with greed.

I made an appointment with the owner and we eventually established a price of 50 cents a ball ($25,000 total). I came up with a contract that would allow me to purchase the balls as I needed them. I also guaranteed the bill would be paid in six months. With this settled, I went instantly to work on the marketing pamphlet. The lead in, or first page, was set up in the following fashion.

Americans spend over $60 billion dollars a year on sports equipment and toys. Sports toys such as the Frisbee and Hoola-Hoop not only fall in the fad category, but they also have become a regular part of the American sports and recreation scene. Frisbee sales have reached a whopping $1 billion and the faddish Hoola-Hoop is sitting at a cool $500 million. Spacebal is fast becoming the Frisbee or Hoola-Hoop of the '90s. Within a short period of time we have sold over a million Spacebals at $4 each. (*This was bullshit.*) Spacebal's patent has been applied for and we expect with our new marketing program to move over 5 million Spacebals in 1992. We want you to become part of our grassroots program. Through our marketing system, the average person (who has always wanted to own a business but could not afford to leave his job security) can now keep his job and become financially independent. If you can afford to spend five hours a week servicing your accounts and collecting money, you can achieve your financial goals.

Our original marketing team cashed in by selling the major chain stores of K-Mart, Osco Drugs, Fred Meyers, Long Drugs, and PayLess. (*Which is more bullshit.*) Sales quickly rocketed to over half a million, but the marketing team soon realized something was wrong. In order to become a Frisbee type of success, Spacebal needed to be marketed — just like the Frisbee — at the smaller, high traffic stores. This was when the business opportunity concept was put together. The idea was to set up private Spacebal distributors in prime areas.

We are looking for people who want to grow with us and are willing to handle Spacebal sports products as well as Spacebal. You, as an independent entrepreneur, can become part of this phenomenon while at the same time becoming monetarily secure. With guaranteed locations, the amount of money you make depends upon how many stores you have. The more you have, the more money you make. (*I would enclose a Projected Profit Sheet similar to the one in Chapter 7.*)

We are not promising that you will make a million overnight, but with the right locations, you will be able to net $2,000 a month with just five displays. The sport of Spacebal will be our next step. Spacebal launchers and catchers will soon be available to our ground floor distributors. These items, along with Spacebal, will make your business venture even more profitable. You, as one of our original distributors, will be the first to handle our new products. Just like Mattel's foundation product, the Barbie doll, and Wham-O Frisbee foundation product, the Frisbee, you can become part of Spacebal's foundation products.

We have all heard people say, "I wish I had purchased a McDonald's franchise (originally a franchise was only $8,000 anywhere in the U.S.) or bought into Polaroid, Coke, Wham-O or Sony." Fortunes have been made by those who had the foresight to do so. Spacebal offers such an opportunity. At present, it is one of the hottest business opportunities on the market.

There is no better time to start. According to Fortune magazine, "a changing economy, abundant support, and a national mood that embraces enterprise make these the best times for launching a business in the U.S."

The truth is that starting a business is less risky than most people think. Among members of the National Federation of Independent Business (an association of small business companies), 77 percent survive the first three years.

Fortune also states that "entrepreneurship (which, in this case, means owning a Spacebal distributorship) suits the way that Americans want to live today" — independent, unsupervised, mobile. People want to choose where they live and work, set their work hours and be their own bosses. By taking on a Spacebal distributorship you are taking on something that may set you up for life. A small investment of your time, money and effort may really pay off in a spectacular way.

WE WANT YOU TO SUCCEED.

Spacebal Newspaper Ads

```
HOT NEW PATENTED SPORTS PRODUCT. Great for the beach. Dis-
tributorship available. Minimum investment 6K. SPACEBAL
Marketing. 1-800-524-6692 203 E. 5th St., Portland, OR
98772
```
(This ad was run in coastal cities.)

```
HOT NEW PATENTED SPORTS PRODUCT. Will replace the FRISBEE.
Distributorship available. Minimum investment 6K. SPACEBAL
Marketing. 1-800-524-6692, 203 E. 5th St., Portland, OR
98772
```
(This ad was run in land-locked cities. Both ads did well.)

Spacebal Phone Pitch

Hello. Are you familiar with the Frisbee and Hoola-Hoop? (Yes. Everyone is.) Well, Spacebal is on the same level as they are. It's a 2-inch rubber ball that has a latex loop running through it. The ball can be shot over 300 feet. We believe that Spacebal will become the Frisbee or Hoola-Hoop of the '90s. We have already sold over a quarter of a million and we anticipate tripling that next year. What we are offering you is a ground floor opportunity to become part of the Spacebal phenomenon. In order to answer a lot of your questions, we would like to C.O.D. you a Fed-Ex package. The package will contain a Spacebal and our marketing pamphlet.

(Keep the phone pitch brief. You want them to accept the C.O.D. material.)

Profit On Spacebal Project

Cost Of Spacebal Project

For this example I will use the LEVEL ONE SPACEBAL Package:

Four floor model spinners — my cost $40 ea. — 4 x 40 =	$ 160.00
Four counter-top spinners — my cost $25 ea. — 4 x 25 =	100.00
1,152 Spacebals — my cost $.50 ea. — 1,152 x $.50 =	576.00
Headers and game pamphlets	50.00
Singers' fees — $20/unit — 20 x 8 displays	160.00
(only if the deal closes)	
1-800-number starter-line	60.00
Business line return calls	125.00
Answering service	45.00
Newspaper ad	185.00
Locating expenses	250.00
(gas, food, motel, etc.)	
Total Costs:	$1,711.00

Spacebal Project Sales

The LEVEL ONE SPACEBAL package included: 4 counter-top spinners, 4 floor spinners, 10 headers, 20 game sheets and 1,152 Spacebals. LEVEL ONE sold for: $6,000.00

Locating fee — $200/unit x 8 units	1,600.00
Total money generated:	7,600.00
Cost of Spacebal project:	1,711.00
PROFIT:	$5,889.00

Chapter 12: Locating

◆ ◆ ◆ ◆ ◆ ◆ ◆ ◆ ◆

Locating is the "wrap," or the last part of your sale. Locating is the placement of the product you have sold. As a biz-op operator, you are offering the mooch a complete package and locating is an important part of that package. "Guaranteed locations" (locations guaranteed to make money or they will be replaced by ones that will) are a powerful closing tool. A mooch will gobble up the promise that his locations are guaranteed to make him money.

It makes no difference if you do the locating or a locating company does. (A list of biz-op locating companies can be found in the REFERENCE chapter.) In order to close your sale, YOU MUST LET THE MOOCH KNOW THAT HIS LOCATIONS ARE GUARANTEED TO MAKE MONEY. That is one of your strongest selling points.

In the Appendix you will find a document that guarantees locations. According to the agreement, you will provide the mooch with "relocates" (new locations) if his product does not sell. Fortunately, "tags" (stipulations that give you ways to break the contract) are written into the agreement. The tags are:

◆ The mooch must provide you with a weekly sales report. (99 percent of the time, a mooch will not continuously send in a weekly sales report, thus making the contract invalid.)
◆ The displays or machines shall be installed within seven days after the locations have been secured. The mooch has to show proof of this. If he cannot, the contract is null and void.
◆ A letter requesting new locations must be sent by certified or registered mail. You, the biz-op operator, must receive the letter no later than the 65th day, otherwise the contract is invalid. If the mooch does not meet all of the above requirements, but still wants new locations, he must pay to have his displays or machines relocated.

After 60 days a mooch knows he has been screwed. The average mooch will say "the hell with it," lick his wounds, and write it off as a bad experience. Unfortunately, you occasionally have a hanger-on who will fulfill all of the location agreement requirements. If he is persistent and keeps calling your service, you can do one of two things. Either change your 1-800-number to a new, unlisted one (providing that you are not in the middle of a project), or have your answering service tell the mooch that you are in the hospital. The mooch will eventually give up.

Locating is the most creative part of the biz-op scam. As I explained earlier, you sell a mooch on a display product by convincing him it is worth more than it actually is.

The only problem with this system is a store owner knows the retail value of the product. Your marketing pamphlet will convince an inexperienced mooch that a $1 bottle of skin cream is worth $7, but trying that with an established store owner is entirely different.

When signing up a store for a display, I use two different forms. The "Independent Location Agreement" and the "Placement Agreement." Both can be found in the Appendix.

If you read these over, you will see that they are "loose," meaning they are very weak legally. The meat of the locating form boils down to this: The location is letting the mooch put his displays in. The displays belong to the mooch. The store owner gets a percentage. If the store wants the display taken out, the mooch must remove it. If the mooch wants to take the display out, he can do so at any time without legal liability. The agreements are simple and non-binding, but it gives the mooch a feeling of security. He now has been accepted by a member of his business community, something he has always wanted. He is independent, free, calling his own shots. He owes it all to you and he is grateful. You are also grateful, especially when he kicks out the greenbacks.

Anyway, back to the problem of slipping an overpriced product into the store of a savvy businessman.

The "Independent Location Agreement" and the "Placement Agreement" forms are custom made for the savvy businessman. Take a good look at both of these forms. THERE IS NO PLACE THAT REQUIRES YOU TO WRITE DOWN THE RETAIL PRICE OF THE PRODUCT. On the "Placement Agreement" form there is a line for "commission." On the "Independent Location Agreement" there is a blank box for "special instructions." Nowhere is there a section devoted to the retail price of the mooch's product. This gives you, the locator, a tremendous advantage. You now have a free hand to verbally state a retail price without writing it down.

Let's say you are dealing with greeting cards. You've gotten a good deal on them by purchasing seconds or close-outs. You have entered into a contract with the mooch to sell him 10,000 cards at 60 cents each. Your cost was 10 cents a card. You have assured the mooch the cards will retail for $1.75. That means if you give the store 50 cents on each card sold, the mooch will end up making 65 cents per card.

Of course you know that the cards are not worth more than 50 cents — unless you are working with an artist biz-op card. (See Chapter 16.) You must now convince stores to take the displays. The first thing you do is go to a Hallmark or any good card store and buy four high quality cards. You glue the back of the cards onto a nice cardboard folder. You do not want the store owner to see the Hallmark name on the back of the cards. The pitch is quick and fast.

"Hi, my name is _____. I'm working with a new, local card company and we're placing small consignment displays of seasonal cards." (Flash the Hallmarks at him.) *"We put them in free of charge."* (Open up one of those spectacular Hallmarks.) *"They retail for $1.25* (instead of $1.75) *and you keep 50 cents for yourself."* (The store owner knows he can easily sell the cards for $1.25.) *"We will come in on a weekly basis to restock the best selling cards."* (If you happen to be placing cards just before a holiday, make sure you have several of those holiday cards. If it's a holiday, tell the owner you are placing displays of that holiday card. Explain how your company will supply all seasonal cards such as Christmas, Easter, etc. The location will be receiving a $500 display at no cost.) *"The only thing we require is this form."* (Hand him the form.) *"It's very loosely written. Basically it states the cards belong to us, but you are to get 50 cents for each one that sells and you can have the display removed at any time."* (After he has read the form, hand him a pen. You should have already filled in the mooch's company name on the "Placement Agreement" and inserted how much the location is to receive for each card they sell.)

Any common sense businessman will see the potential of getting something for nothing. There is no risk involved.

By using the "Placement Agreement" form, you do not expose the retail price of the product. When the mooch looks at the "Placement Agreement" he only sees the 50-cent commission. He has no idea you have told the store owner his $1.75 cards are going to sell for $1.25.

After you have completed the agreed number of contracts, list all the stores on the LOCATION LIST. (See the Appendix.) The bottom of the LOCATION LIST form reads: "I hereby acknowledge receipt of a copy of the list of locations from my route of _____ (Insert the product. In this case it would be 10 greeting cards displays.) with the understanding that no guarantee of profit is made or implied by the seller and that all commitments made by _____ (your company name) have been complied with. I am satisfied with the locations and am aware that I may change locations if I should desire." You then have the mooch. Sign it and initial next to "I have toured these locations."

Touring the locations is always tricky. One golden rule of the tour is NEVER LET THE MOOCH HAVE AN IN DEPTH CONVERSATION WITH THE LOCATION OWNER.

I have two effective ways of accomplishing this. Since your mooch is a novice entrepreneur, he needs your advice. You are a teacher: he is the student. Using this kind of power, you pre-warn the mooch that business owners do not like to be disturbed. Tell the mooch you had to set up an appointment before you could talk to the store owner. Explain that, "In order to stay in the owner's good graces, we only want to pop in and out." By using this pre-warning ploy, you eliminate the chance of the mooch staying around and chatting about the cards.

The other way of speeding up the tour is to use only one car, yours. I always insist that we take my automobile. By controlling the tempo of the drive time, you effectively keep the mooch from loitering. When the tour is finished, stop at a McDonald's or a bright little coffee shop. Get the paperwork signed. Give the mooch a carbon-less notebook. (He will use this when delivering the cards. Someone in the store must sign for the card inventory.) Then collect the rest of your money. In this case the remaining amount due on 10 card displays is $1,500. It must be paid by either cash or money order. NEVER ACCEPT A PERSONAL CHECK.

Aftermath

Most of the time, a mooch will get his displays installed. It is usually by mistake or luck. The store owner might be too busy to look at the display and he will just point to an area and say, "Put it over there." Sometimes the store owner will be out when the mooch drops the display off. Other times the store owner will just feel sorry for the mooch and let him leave it. It makes little difference. Usually after 30 days the store owners will want the displays taken out.

If you are a smart biz-op operator, you will get the mooch a "backup" location. There is a good chance the store owner might turn down the card display. Backup locations can alleviate excess mooch bitching. Hopefully this will do the trick. If not, all hell will break loose and you will need to have your 1-800-number changed to a new, unlisted one. That means the only way the mooch has of contacting you is through your PO Box. After 30 days he will tire of sending you nasty letters.

Chapter 13:
Vending

♦ ♦ ♦ ♦ ♦ ♦ ♦ ♦ ♦

Snack vending is the backbone of business opportunities marketing. When I started biz-opping, vending was my primary source of income. New biz-oppers still cut their teeth on honor boxes and candy vending machines.

Vending has been around longer than Christianity. The first vend popped up in 215 B.C. It was a primitive vend that reacted to the weight of a coin and spilled out a small amount of holy water. Since that time, inventors and biz-oppers have created a business that is currently grossing over $10 billion annually. Vending machines now spit out everything from frozen steaks to hot, by-the-slice pizza.

Candy vending accounts for 80 percent of the solid food vends. There are bulk vends that dispense handfuls of nuts, countertop vends that kick out full-size candy bars, compact vends that hold bite-size candy bars, and vends with built in microwaves that not only give you candy, but pop popcorn as well. (See REFERENCE chapter for a list of manufacturers.)

Your vending machine newspaper ad plays an important part in vending sales. It must be more interesting than other ads. Here are samples of successful vending machine ads.

```
SNACK ROUTE. Newest and most profitable snack machines are
opening up hundreds of new locations. Seeing is believing.
Earnings can exceed $1,000 weekly. Part time. All cash busi-
ness can be yours for as little as $5,600. Call 1-800-
```

```
$ SUCCESS IN 1994 $. Unlike anything you've ever seen, the
hottest little vending machine is sweeping the nation. This is
an incredible opportunity to secure your financial future. To-
tally recession-proof. No experience needed. No selling. Deal
only with highly established accounts. Fantastic profits, part
or full time. Be the first in your area with our proven money-
maker. If you are sincere about your financial future, contact
us today for a color pamphlet. Investment of $3,600 opens your
```

```
chain of instant profit centers. Call 1-800- to get in on this
ground floor opportunity.

BEST ONE MAN BUSINESS EVER. U.S.A.'s number one money-maker in
automatic merchandising. It's hot! It's here now! It can make
you independent. No selling. No overhead. Start part time. Ap-
prox. 4 hrs./wk. Investment required $15,950. Limited opportu-
nity. Call 24 hours for brochure. 1-800-

SNACK ROUTE. Established locations. Profitability guaranteed.
$800/week cash income. Call 24 hours for free brochure. 1-800-
```

The last ad promises an established candy vending route. It gives the impression that the machines are in place and making money. The ad is called a "grabber," something that will get the mooch on the telephone. Once he's on line, ask what city he lives in. Then explain that you have 10 great locations (in his area) that want vending machines. These locations are so good that he will make $800 a week. All he has to do is purchase the vends, place them in the high grossing locations, and start making money.

This is your primary lead in pitch for an established vending route ad. When you run an established vending route ad, the locations are included. Because of this, you will have to up the price of the vending machine to compensate for the locating fee.

After closing one of these deals, you will have to hustle. The locations should be ready before the machines are sent. If not, don't worry about it. As long as you have the mooch's money, he is at your mercy. When using the established route ad, have the machines in stock. On the other ads, you can wait until you have the mooch's money before purchasing the vends.

Countertop Vending Machine
Weight: 85 lb.
Size: 30" × 20" × 22"
Capacity: 185 items

Big Buck Brand Mechanical Countertop Vending Machine

Play around with different vending ads. See which one works best for you. I occasionally run two different ads in the same paper. It's interesting when the same mooch responds to both ads. You know right away that you have an "air-head" on line.

Today there is a glut of vending machines. Manufacturers are producing and selling vends at a record rate. Selling the machines is not a problem. The only difficulty is locations, but that can be easily overcome by using charities. (See Chapter 6.) If you study Chapter 6 and the charity forms in the Appendix, you can locate from 5 to 10 machines a day.

There is an art to purchasing vending machines. The best buys are used machines from your previous mooches. Always keep a mooch hit list, a list of all people to whom you have sold vending machines. (Do not worry about any of the following until you have built up a mooch hit list.) 70 percent of your mooches will want to unload their machines within one year. Driving from business to business to put in one candy bar quickly changes their vision of the billion-dollar vending industry. That's where you once again step in. Only this time the mooch doesn't know who you are. You will need to get another mailbox and 1-800-number. Do not use your old PO Box or 1-800-number. Even a half-witted mooch will recognize the address and phone number of the person who "dry humped him."

Put together a mass mail postcard. You are now going to become a buyer of used vending machines. I call my company Vending Liquidators of America. The name is boldly printed on both the front and back of the postcard. (Do not use a PO Box number, only a suite address.) The rest of the postcard reads: "WE BUY ALL USED VENDING MACHINES, COUNTERTOPS, UPRIGHT VENDS, MICRO VENDS, ETC. CALL FOR INSTANT CASH. 1-800-"

Since the mooch will recognize your voice, make arrangements with your answering service to give out the information. There will be an additional charge, but it keeps you out of the picture. (Instruct the answering service not to give your name, only your company's name.) The answering service is to ask what type of machine it is, if it is in good shape, and how old it is. Authorize them to quote these prices: $75 for countertops, $200 for upright vends, and $300 for microwave vends. The mooch is to re-pack the vends and have them sent C.O.D. will-call to your specified U.P.S. terminal. Try to get him to pay the freight. If he bitches, you'll have to pay.

When they arrive, check the weight of the boxes. Countertops will weigh 85 pounds; microwave vends 158 pounds. If the U.P.S. form indicates the weight is different, ask for one of the boxes to be opened. If they refuse, do not accept the shipment. The mooch who sent the machines expects to be paid by cashier's check. There is nothing wrong with this, but protect yourself. Once you have checked the weight and given U.P.S. the cashier's check, you had better act quickly. Open the boxes. If the "mooch" has sent you badly damaged machines, then re-tape the boxes and give them back to U.P.S. At that time, make a mad dash to your bank and have them cancel the cashier's check. Most people are unaware of this, but your bank can stop payment on a cashier's check. Especially if you tell them it's to prevent an attempted fraud.

Until you have compiled a mooch hit list, you will have to rely on classifieds and manufacturers for your vending machines. If you are a serious biz-opper, the classifieds will become your second Bible. You have to devote time to the classifieds. Read them daily. You never know when a hidden money-maker will pop up. Many a time I have practically stolen used vending machines advertised in the classifieds. A desperate mooch will sometimes take almost any offer to get rid of his vending machine burden. Another classified vending method is the vending purchasing ad. "LOOKING FOR USED VENDING MACHINES. WILL PAY CASH. Phone #." This ad will sometimes create more business than you can handle.

Always check the mechanics and condition of the vends. For countertops offer $75 to $120, for upright vends $150 to $200, for microwave vends $200 to $500, and for hot food vends offer $200 to $300.

Your last option is the manufacturer. Even though the prices are structured to let you make good money, your net profit will not be nearly as much as on the used machines. A list of vending manufacturers and prices of their machines can be found in the REFERENCE chapter.

Profit On Vending Machine Project

I am going to work with the most popular vend, the countertop. The package will be 10 used machines. Very seldom will the mechanism in a manual vending machine give you trouble. If a coin mechanism goes out, just order a replacement. Most of the used machines will need to be touched up and polished. It only takes a little work to make a vend look brand new. If at all possible, keep the machines in the original boxes. If not, buy good, sturdy, nice-looking shipping containers.

Vending Machine Project Costs
(10 Countertops)

Cost of 10 used vends: $75 x 10 =	$750.00
Cost of refurbishing — spray paint, steel wool:	30.00
(you can have it done by professional appliance repair person)	
Shipping boxes (good ones): $10 x 10 =	100.00
Singer fee: $20 a unit x 10 = $200 x 2 singers =	400.00
(only if deal closes)	
1-800-number starter-line:	50.00
Business line return calls:	100.00
Answering service:	45.00
Newspaper ad:	175.00
Locating expenses:	250.00
(gas, food, motel, etc.)	
Total Costs:	$1,900.00

Vending Project Profit

10 Countertops @ $600 =	$6,000.00
Locating fee, $100/unit =	1,000.00
Total Sale:	$7,000.00
Total Costs =	$1,900.00
PROFIT:	$5,100.00

If you run a week-long ad, you should close three vending packages, for a total profit of $15,300.00.

The pitch on the vending machines is similar to that for the honor boxes. (See Chapter 8.) Ask the mooch if he would like to make $800 a week with only 4 hours of work. He will have an exclusive distributorship, a ground floor opportunity — all of your distributors are making money — and he will be guaranteed to make money or the machines will be moved. The mooch will be taken around and introduced to the store or company owner.

It doesn't have to be a long or complicated pitch. Go for the greed factor. The mooch is calling because he is hoping to go into business and get rich. Tell him what he wants to hear.

Here's the lead-in to your profit pamphlet:

Dear _____,

Here is the pamphlet you requested regarding the billion dollar world of vending. Each day, millions of coins are poured through coin-operated devices. Automatic merchandising is one of today's fastest growing industries. Everyday nearly 7 out of 10 persons will do business with automatic merchandisers. The fantastic potential for this business has only begun to be fully realized.

Not only is the greatest growth of vending ahead of us, but also the greatest diversification of vending is yet to come.

Here are a few reasons why automatic merchandising is practically exploding. The high cost of labor in personal selling activities makes automatic vending a more interesting alternative. Vending machines can operate virtually anywhere and at anytime. The trends towards more impulse purchasing by consumers will benefit the growth of this industry.

Our compact countertop meets the huge demand by thousands of businesses that do not have the floor space for large floor models. Our countertop is 100 percent mechanical, requiring no costly repairs. It costs far less than electronic machines. It holds up to 175 items and resembles fine office furniture. In America total snack sales are over $19 billion and growing 10 percent annually. You can have a piece of the vending pie.

At present, our vending company is working with a select number of distributors. Each of our distributors runs a profitable operation and we are looking for more distributors to join our family.

Please go over all the enclosed profit material and a representative will call on you with information on distributors who are becoming financially independent.

Chapter 14: Auctions

◆ ◆ ◆ ◆ ◆ ◆ ◆ ◆ ◆

Government auctions present excellent opportunities for biz-oppers. The government sells over $1 billion in surplus every year. My most profitable biz-op government auction deal involved the purchase of 100 microwaves. (See Chapter 17.)

The major drawback to auctions is cash. If you are just starting, and short of cash, auctions might be beyond your means. I have put together a complete list of things you need to know about auctions.

Once you have decided to attend one, make sure you know how to get to the location. Drive by before the auction, check out parking and see how to get inside. This eliminates some possible reasons for being late when the time comes.

Get there early enough to inspect the merchandise. There is usually an open inspection period that will allow you to look at the goods. Sometimes the inspection takes place the day before the auction. Always ask. If you are after biz-op items, make sure they fall into the biz-op merchandising category. REMEMBER, at an auction all sales are final.

When bidding for an item, make eye contact with the auctioneer. This will let him know you are a serious bidder. Make sure you know the bidding amount of the item you are interested in. If you are unsure, ask the auctioneer to repeat the amount. Auctioneers speak rapidly, so don't get confused and buy something for more than you intended.

At government auctions, no deposit is required to bid. If you make a purchase, you must make a partial payment of 20 percent of the total amount. (Unless full payment is required.) Full payment will be accepted in the form of cash or money order. No personal checks.

Government auctions are supervised by the General Services Administration (G.S.A.). See REFERENCE chapter for the G.S.A. office closest to you. Also in the REFERENCE chapter is a complete list of the government's Defense Re-utilization and Marketing regional sales offices.

There are two other government auctions — neither is too much benefit to the biz-opper — merchandise seized by drug enforcement and the U.S. Customs. These items are sold at sealed bid auctions. A sealed bid is just like an auction, except the bids are placed in an envelope by the bidder, sealed, and turned over to the auctioneer, who opens the envelopes. The merchandise is then awarded to the highest bidder. The items auctioned usually include liquor, jewelry, boats, airplanes, automobiles, real estate, clothing items and household goods — very few things that a biz-opper can work with, mainly personal things at a very low price. Although these auctions are open to anyone, you must become a member/subscriber to participate in the auction. To become a member/subscriber, contact: EG&G, 55 Bodega Drive, Nogales, AZ 85621, (602) 281-4705. This company is under contract with the U.S. government to conduct the customs and drug seizure auctions. Send them a stamped, self-addressed envelope and they will send you an application.

Other auctions that I have done extremely well with are the bank and financial auctions. I bid on and got 100,000 boxed bottles of Rain Forest skin lotion and hair cream — a horrible product from the rain forest of Costa Rica that turned out to be a great money maker. (See Chapter 15.)

Bank auctions are held because companies or individuals can no longer meet their financial commitments. In order to recoup some of their money, the banks have an auction. This means a biz-opper can get a great discount on money making items. These auctions are held about every two weeks, depending on how long the institutions want to hold the merchandise.

Where do you find these auctions? First look in the Yellow Pages under Banks, Credit Unions, and Finance Companies. Call them and ask when the next auction of repossessed property will be held. They will tell you the time and date. Also check the classifieds in the local paper and in *U.S.A. Today*.

When you get to an auction and you have been declared the high bidder, proceed to the cashier's table. You must pay at least $150 on your purchase price before the end of the auction. This is a deposit on your merchandise. You will then have seven days to pay the balance. (Be sure to keep the receipt for your deposit.) If the balance is not paid in the specified time, you lose your deposit and the merchandise is auctioned off again.

Chapter 15: Rain Forest

◆ ◆ ◆ ◆ ◆ ◆ ◆ ◆ ◆

Bank auctions can sometimes lead to unexpected wealth, as in the case of Rain Forest. I was working a mooch in Florida and, as always, I picked up the local paper and checked out the classifieds. Under Auctions, I found that the Bank of Carney was auctioning off several different lots of repossessed items. I called and discovered one lot contained skin care products.

There was a combination of 100,000 bars of soap, and bottles of skin cream and hair cream. A cosmetic company called Rain Forest had imported the product from Costa Rica. According to what I could glean from the literature, all the ingredients were from the Costa Rican rain forest. I opened up several bottles and wasn't impressed. It was poorly packaged and the bottles were of a cheap rubber composition. The skin cream reminded me more of white axle grease than skin lotion. I could see why it didn't sell. That made little difference. If the price was right, I knew it could be biz-opped for a tidy profit.

Included in the lot were 1,000 empty small sample jars labeled Rain Forest and approximately 900 cheap, thin-pressed wood displays. The displays were not much more than firewood, but that was all I needed. Those items combined with the bottled axle grease would be the key to the Rain Forest project.

My bid of $5,000 got the whole lot. My cost per unit was five cents. The displays were just thrown in as part of the package.

There were three different products — hair repairing cream, cleansing bars, and skin cream. I decided to go with packages of 12 and 25 units. The big package would include 25 displays with 1,000 bottles of hair cream, 1,000 bars of Rain Forest soap, and 1,200 bottles of skin cream. I had enough product to sell approximately 35 big packages.

We rented an office storage space in Tampa and set up shop. Our first marketing step was to purchase enough good quality skin cream to fill up the 1,000 sample containers. Next we found a high-quality wooden display. With display in hand, we went to a Sears family photo studio. At that time, Sears was having one of their specials where you and the kids sit in front of a pull-down backdrop for a snapshot. Our chosen backdrop was a waterfall. For the family, we substituted a Rain Forest display. For $29.95 we ended up with a nice cover photo for the Rain Forest marketing pamphlet. We then joined the Better Business Bureau. The B.B.B. can be a real asset when you are working on a long-term project. Since your company is new, the B.B.B. will not have any complaints. That gives you bonus mooch points. A mooch always feels more comfortable when the B.B.B. verifies that your company is complaint-free.

One of the things you must do when working with a cheap, worthless product is create the brand name illusion. You want to convince the mooch that this product is as good as Estee Lauder. The only reason it is being sold for less is that people are not familiar with it. It also creates a consumer friendly attitude. Instead of paying $60 an ounce for Estee Lauder, they can now buy a product that is comparable, Rain Forest, at $6 an ounce.

To help enhance Rain Forest's image, we put together a list of the best skin lotions in the world. Naturally, the list included our bottled axle grease. This list helped plant the seed in the mooch's mind that Rain Forest skin cream was as good as any big-name product.

Facial Skin Care and Hair Care Products Represent

A $4 Billion a Year Market In The U.S.

This is a List of The Very Best

Brand Name	Size	Retail Price
Healing Skin Creams		
1. Lancome Anti-Aging Cream	1.75 oz.	$35
2. Biotherm Wrinkle Smoother	1.37 oz.	$32
3. Prescriptives Multi Moisturizer	1.09 oz.	$37
4. Estee Lauder Controlling Cream	1.75 oz.	$60
5. La Prairie Creme Cellular	1 oz.	$80
6. Ultima II All Night Moisturizer	1 oz.	$40
7. Shiseido Facial Nourishing Cream	1 oz.	$37
8. Princess Marcella Borghese	1.85 oz.	$25
9. Elizabeth Arden Day Renewal Emulsion	1.75 oz.	$52
10. Clinique Daytime Moisturizer	1.75 oz.	$37
11. RAIN FOREST NATURAL PRODUCTS CREAM 2 ounces $$$$$$ 12.95! ! ! ! !		

Miracle skin creams are in abundance. Claims of getting rid of wrinkles and old age blotches are as common as apple pie. Everyone wants to stay young. The mooch can relate to this. He also realizes that skin creams are expensive. Many people may want high-priced skin cream, but cannot afford it. But now, thanks to the Rain Forest distributor, the dreams of the average working woman can be fulfilled. Beauty and youth will be hers forever.

Rain Forest Newspaper Ads

```
$ UNLIMITED $$$$$. New! All-natural skin products. More
advanced than Estee Lauder. Ground Floor Opportunity. RAIN
FOREST — the COSMETIC WAVE OF THE FUTURE CALL -

A+$UPER DOLLAR$. Billion dollar industry. NEW!! HOT! All
natural skin product. Exclusive distributorship — $10K
required. RAIN FOREST - Call

MAKE $200,000 A YEAR!! Own a natural cosmetic business.
NEW. Exclusive distributorship — No experience necessary
— $10K RAIN FOREST — Call
```

The Rain Forest phone pitch will sound familiar. (That's because all the pitches have the same format.)

Hi _____

Are you familiar with Estee Lauder and Max Factor? (Yes, everybody is.) What we are offering is a product that is on the same level, if not above, Estee Lauder. We have spent millions of dollars on research. It has taken years to perfect an all-natural product of this nature and we have finally gotten the O.K. to begin our marketing in the United States. We do not want the skin cream to be mass marketed in chain stores such as KMart or Wal-Mart. We want to set up distributors who will have an exclusive territory. They, in turn, will get this fabulous new product into the hands of the independent beauty shops, tanning salons, dermatologists, etc. — shops that work one on one with their customers.

The skin cosmetics business grossed over $4 billion last year and Rain Forest is going to be taking a big piece of the pie. The distributors that get in on this ground floor opportunity are going to make money. If this is something you're interested in, we would like to C.O.D. you a Fed-Ex package of information.

Marketing Pamphlet First Page

I used some of the literature that the old Rain Forest company had put together. A lot of it is a low-key, product pushing, soft sell. I incorporated it with some of my own hype and this is what I came up with.

Dear _____,

We appreciate your response to RAIN FOREST, THE NATURAL COSMETIC WAVE OF THE FUTURE. Rain Forest Products has developed the most advanced beauty system available anywhere in the world. Our rare and active ingredients are obtained deep inside the rain forest in Central America. Our natural, patented formulas are the premise to an entire line of all-natural skin and hair care products.

We are acquiring high quality, all-natural ingredients from the incredible Costa Rican rain forest and trying to help re-flourish the destroyed area. We always try to avoid use of industrialized ingredients, but in some cases it is necessary to include a minimum amount of some stabilizer or preservatives. *(I personally thought they got the ingredients from a South American rubber factory.)*

We have spent many years improving our techniques to achieve the most natural product. We are now sure that our line is one of the best for people who appreciate natural products. Our soaps and creams are manufactured with absolutely traditional procedures, using ancient techniques to maintain their unique quality.

Our line is the result of years of experimenting with raw and rough ingredients like herbal powders, infusions, oils, extracts, concentrates, mud, clay, sea elements, etc.

We are now offering distributorships to a few selected people. Those who become part of our family will be on the same level as the first Max Factor or Coca-Cola distributor. Stop and think. How many people do you know who made an $8,000 investment in the first McDonald's franchise? Not too many. (McDonald's franchises are now $1 million.) That's because it takes people with insight who are willing to take that first entrepreneurial step. Those with that insight will be America's next millionaires.

Are you one of those people? We have the product and we want dependable distributors who are visionaries to handle Rain Forest. Our professional locators will secure the highest quality places for the Rain Forest displays. All our distributors have to do is restock (which you will be doing a lot of), drop off literature, see if the shop owner has any questions, and THEN COLLECT YOUR MONEY. What could be simpler?

You have a chance to become part of a ground floor operation in an industry that grosses over $4 billion annually. This opportunity may never come along again.

Try the sample that we have enclosed. I'm sure you will agree that it is the best skin cream in America. *(It was.)* Then carefully read over the enclosed material. In a few days, we will call back with information on other distributors who, for a $10,000 investment, have reached their financial goals. The American dream for them is a reality — just as it can be for you.

Profit On Rain Forest Project

Cost Of Rain Forest Project

I sold two different packages. One package had 12 units, the other 25. In this example we will use a package of 25. I will also include the cost of my "plant" (See Chapter 5) as well as the Sears pictures, wooden display and cost of a good skin cream. These items are a one time only expense. On a big money project, we went to national as well as local papers. All the expenses will be higher than normal.
(Based on packages of 25)

- Rain Forest skin cream. The "mooch" receives 1,250 assorted skin creams. My cost: $62.50.
- Rain Forest hair cream. The "mooch" receives 1,000 units. My cost: $50.
- Rain Forest cleansing bars. The "mooch" receives 1,000 units. My cost: $50.
- Cost of marketing pamphlet, color covers and 500 pamphlets for the mooch to hand out: $225.
- *USA Today* advertising: $475/week.
- Local newspaper advertising, California and Texas: $350.
- 1-800-number incoming calls: $145
- Business line (going out): $350.
- Answering service: $125.
- Singers — two singers were paid $50/unit to set up a total of 24 "plants" (See Chapter 5.) $1,200. The singers were then paid $20/unit to tell the mooch how great Rain Forest sales were. Two singers x 50 units x $20 = $2,000.
- Cost of skin cream to fill the empty sample bottles: $340.
- Nice wooden display: $125.
- Sears photos: $29.95.
- Locating expense (25 units). Motel, gas, food, etc. $350.

Summary:

Skin cream	62.50
Hair cream	50.00
Soap	50.00
Printing	225.00
USA Today ads	475.00
Local paper ads	350.00
1 -800 #	145.00
Business line	350.00
Answering service	125.00
Singers	3,200.00
Good skin cream	340.00
Display	125.00
Photos	29.95
Locating expense	350.00
Total Costs:	$5,877.45

Profit On Rain Forest Project

Rain Forest skin cream — 1,250 containers at $5.77 ea. = $7,212.50.
Rain Forest hair cream — 1,000 containers at $3.99 ea. =   3,990.00
Rain Forest soap — 1,000 bars at $1.45 =   1,450.00
25 Rain Forest deluxe displays $229 ea. =   5,720.00
Locating fee $250/unit x 25 =   6,250.00
                                                        _____
Total: $24,622.50
Cost of Product: 5,877.45
PROFIT: $18,745.05

We ended up having enough product to sell 30 packages. After that, we shut down and I beat a hot path out of Florida. My partners and I netted almost half a million in six months.

The REFERENCE chapter has a list of cosmetic companies you can purchase discontinued items from. Most of the time you will have to create a new name for the product and have new labels made for each bottle.

Chapter 16: Greeting Cards

◆ ◆ ◆ ◆ ◆ ◆ ◆ ◆ ◆

There is hardly a person alive who has not received a greeting card. Everyone knows that cards are a profitable, big business. Just look at Hallmark and Carrollton. A $2 card has a buck and a half of profit in it. It's this "fat money" that makes Hallmark big, but it's the mooch's fat money that makes the biz-op operator big.

If you are going to run a greeting card ad, you need to find a card source. Good sources are stores that are bankrupt or going out of business. A biz-opper has to be a continual classified ad watcher. It's in the classifieds that you find good deals — drugstores going under, stationery or grocery stores closing. These are things that suddenly pop up in your local paper. One week there will be a bankruptcy auction, the next week everything will be sold. If you are looking to pick up auction bankruptcy cards, you must continually scan the paper. You should never pay more than one to two cents a card at an auction. Your price to the mooch is 50 cents a card.

There are easier ways of locating cards than at an auction. One is purchasing seconds, or close-outs, that the big card companies have. (There is a list in the REFERENCE chapter.) The best way to approach these companies is with a letter. Here is the correspondence I send requesting seconds or close-outs:

Big Time Marketing
Seattle, WA

American Greeting Cards
Cleveland, OH
Attn: Sales Dept.

Our company represents a chain of 99-cent stores in the Northwest. Our client has requested a larger selection of greeting cards. We realize that American Greeting cards are of a high quality and we do not expect them to give us a top of the line card. What we are searching for are seconds and close-outs. We do not care if the cards have blemishes, but we would like seasonal cards (X-mas, Easter, etc.), as well as the traditional birthday and get-wells. We need to purchase them in lots of 5,000 to 10,000. People do not expect high quality in 99-cent stores, but we will naturally need envelopes and, if at all possible, headers for the spinners. We would appreciate a reply within 30 days. If you have any questions, please call 999-999-. Thank you.

(You can use a variation of this formatted letter with cosmetic companies, seed companies and automotive companies.)

Almost every card company will come up with something. Always keep the price at 10 cents a card or less. Remember, you have to pay for these up front; the "sell then buy" method will not work.

The least expensive way (the way I like most) of biz-opping cards is the local artist route. If you know an artist or a cartoonist who is willing to put together a series of 24 different greeting cards on a percentage basis, go for it. Providing, of course, the artist is half decent.

I worked with an Hispanic college artist who was exceptional. He put together a series of cards that appealed to the Spanish population. I sold 10 different distributorships in California, Texas, and Arizona. All of his artwork was of a Spanish cartoon theme done in black and white. I produced samples by going to the local quick printer. There I instructed the printer to make copies of the cards on a high quality, heavy duty gloss paper. After the copies were run, I precisely cut and folded them. Twenty complete sets were made. One was for the artist, one was for myself, and the rest were mooch bait. Since I was using quality paper and only running 480 copies, I paid 15 cents each. The price dropped to 7 cents each when I ordered 5,000.

You must always work out the percentage agreement with the artist before entering in a biz-op artist deal. Even if he is a friend, put it in writing. If he doesn't create cards that look decent, no one makes money. All he has to do is create a mooch card. It needs to have a character or scene that you can sell as being your trademark. No one else has this card and your mooch will be the only one in his territory to have it. My Hispanic artist created a crazy rabbit. All of the text was in Spanish and in English.

My agreement with the artist guaranteed that he would receive 7 cents for each card sold. On a five-display deal (5,000 cards), his percentage was $350. A card package always starts at five units. It consists of five floor model card spinners that hold 45 different cards, 5,000 cards (1,000 per display) and five headers.

If you are purchasing cards at an auction, the spinners might be included. If not, there are several different ways of tracking down spinners. One is to call all the local grocery and drugstores. Ask if they have any used spinners they want to get rid of. If they do, make sure the spinners are sized to fit your cards. Never give more than $20 for a used spinner.

One drugstore actually gave me 10 aluminum greeting card displays just to make more room in their storage area. I took the spinners to a sandblasting shop and had the old paint removed. The next stop was at an auto paint shop for a quick glossy-white coat. Sandblasting $125, painting $200, total $325. A beginning biz-opper can save money by using a little elbow grease, sandpaper and canned spray paint.

If you cannot find used displays, check in the Yellow Pages under Grocery-Drugstore Displays or Showroom Displays. You should be able to find what you want, but it might be too expensive. The cheapest route is to go mail order with Siegel Displays. (See REFERENCE chapter.) Twenty card spinners will cost you $60 each. You always want to triple the highest wholesale price of the displays. If they are $60, you charge the mooch $180.

As far as the cards go, you need to wholesale them at 50 cents each. Anything above that might scare your mooch off.

If you are printing a local artist card, you should be able to produce them for 16½ cents a piece. That includes the artist's fee, printing and an envelope. I have gotten cards at an auction for as low as two cents, but everything at an auction is cash. The same is true of the Hallmark type of close outs. The big drawback to company and auction cards is you have the cards before you have bagged the mooch. With artist biz-op cards, you pay for the cards with the mooch's money.

Complete Displays

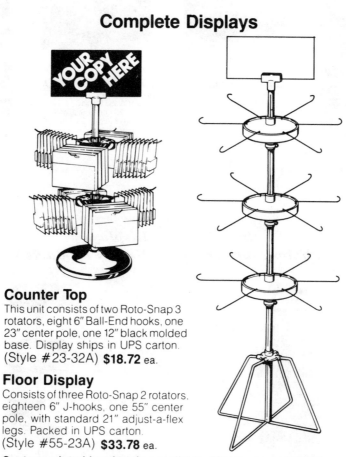

Counter Top
This unit consists of two Roto-Snap 3 rotators, eight 6" Ball-End hooks, one 23" center pole, one 12" black molded base. Display ships in UPS carton. (Style #23-32A) **$18.72** ea.

Floor Display
Consists of three Roto-Snap 2 rotators, eighteen 6" J-hooks, one 55" center pole, with standard 21" adjust-a-flex legs. Packed in UPS carton. (Style #55-23A) **$33.78** ea.

Custom printed header sign available. Minimum quantity 60.

Product Displays
(Illustrations courtesy Siegel Display Products)

GREETING CARD DISPLAYS

Gives your cards great visibility in a minimum of space. Pockets show full view of cards and hold 2 doz. cards w/ envelopes. Sloping bottom of pocket prevents cards from slumping. Pocket assemblies on floor models are interchangeable. Made of steel with durable, white epoxy powder coating. Assembles in minutes – without tools! Rotates on ball bearings and has 5 leg tubular steel base for strength and stability.

AR19

COUNTER TOP DISPLAYS
AR17: 16 Pocket 5 X 7
AR18: 16 Pocket Studio
AR19: 24 Pocket 5 x 7

AR13

DOUBLE SPINNER DISPLAY
AR13: 8-18 Pocket Wings
AR14: Combo Display
　　　 4-20 Pocket Studio Wings
　　　 4-18 Pocket 5 x 7 Wings

AR6

STUDIO CARD SPINNER
AR7: 1-20 Pocket Studio Wing
　　　 3-18 Pocket 5 x 7 Wings
AR5: 3-20 Pocket Wings
AR6: 4-20 Pocket Studio Wings

AR4

5 x 7 CARD SPINNER - FLOOR
AR4: 4-18 Pocket Wings
AR2: 4-12 Pocket Wings
AR1: 3-12 Pocket Wings

Greeting Card Displays
(Photos courtesy Siegel Display Products.)

Two Versions of Seed Spinners
(Illustrations courtesy Siegel Display Products.)

This is the lead in I used for the marketing pamphlet:

Dear_____,

Thanks for your interest in our exclusive greeting card distributorship. Our unique, attractive cards were the hit of the Atlanta card show.

If you are a new entrepreneur, you need to know four things about cards:

1. How safe is my investment?

2. Who is in the business now?

3. How much are they making?

4. Can I reasonably expect to do as well or better?

Those are really important questions and the enclosed material has the answers. You'll find facts, figures and specific information.

With Hispanic Creations, you will have the best of several worlds — money, success, enjoyment and — perhaps the greatest gift of all — complete independence.

Our distributors require no special skills in sales, bookkeeping or technical training to manage their business. No heavy lifting is involved. All that's required is a desire to be financially successful.

If there is one thing you can say about successful people it is that they open the door when opportunity knocks. Our distributorship is knocking really loud. You are looking for the best business you can find; we are searching for the best sellers in your area.

We appreciate your interest. Now, carefully review the facts and figures in the enclosed material. Go off by yourself where it's quiet and read it from cover to cover. You'll see why cards by Hispanic Creations are a success. You'll discover why, as a grassroots distributor, you have the same opportunity as the first Coca-Cola distributor.

Analyze the information today. Make notes about any questions you may have. We will call you back within the next few days and respond to any questions you have.

Should you want answers before we call, use our toll free line, 1-800-, and ask for _____. You will now have the opportunity to join the satisfied family of Hispanic Creations. OUR DISTRIBUTORS DO NOT ANSWER TO A SUPERVISOR OR BOSS. THEY CHOOSE THEIR OWN WORKING HOURS. PART TIME OR FULL TIME. THEY ARE ASSOCIATED WITH AN INDUSTRY THAT IS EXCITING AND TRULY REWARDING.

Best of all, you can be up and running in a few weeks. But don't hesitate too long. We have received inquiries from many, many persons who responded to the same newspaper advertisement in your area.

The next time we speak on the phone, I'll give you the names and phone numbers of some of our dealers. This will enable you to get an overall picture of the success of Hispanic Creations.

Profit On Greeting Card Project

Cost Of Greeting Card Project:

(Based on a 10-spinner biz-op artist package using reconditioned spinners.)
Cost of printing cards (black and white on good gloss paper):

8 cents ea. x 10,000 =	$ 800.00
Cost of 10 reconditioned displays: =	350.00
Singers' fees: $20 a display x 10 x 3 singers =	600.00
(only to be paid if deal closes)	
Artist's percentage: 7 cents x 10,000 cards =	700.00
Answering service:	45.00
1-800-number starter-line: should not be over	60.00
Business line return calls: should not be over	85.00
Newspaper ad:	175.00
Locating expenses — gas, food, motel, etc.:	250.00
Total Costs:	$3,065.00

Money Taken In On Card Project

10,000 cards x 50 cents =	$ 5,000.00
10 spinners x $240 =	2,400.00
Locating fee — 10 x $300 =	3,000.00
Total money generated:	$10,400.00
Cost of project:	$3,065.00
PROFIT:	$7,335.00

Successful Newspaper Ads

I ran the Hispanic ad in several Spanish newspapers. We sold two distributorships, but I had to hire a person fluent in Spanish. For card locating pitch, see Chapter 12.

Chapter 17:
Popcorn

◆ ◆ ◆ ◆ ◆ ◆ ◆ ◆ ◆

Auctions make biz-oppers money. Unfortunately, you must have cash. The "sell then buy" method does not work with auctions. There is a risk factor involved when purchasing items before selling them. I suggest new biz-oppers stay with the "sell then buy" method until they have become more experienced.

One of my most successful government auctions involved microwaves. The horror stories you hear about the government spending $500 on a hammer or $800 on toilet seats must be true. I bid on and purchased 100 small commercial Litton microwaves for $3,000. At that time it was the smallest commercial microwave Litton made: 13 inches x 18 inches x 9 inches high, .5 cu. ft. interior, 700 watts of power; weight 37 lbs. It retailed for $200. I do not know what the government paid, but my per unit cost was $30. (Litton is no longer making that model.) I have sold and purchased many coin-operated large microwave vending machines, but this project would be a little different.

My first move was to contact Deli Express (Eden Prairie, MN, 1-800-328-8184) and work a deal to purchase 1,000 cases of their assorted microwave popcorn. There are 48 packs of popcorn per case. My cost per case was $6.50. Without purchasing the popcorn, I began running my ads. The object was to sell microwave popcorn routes.

The microwave popcorn ads read:

```
$ 114% PROFIT $. Phenomenal return on investment. $3,500
required. #1 selling snack food. CALL -

ONLY $3,500!!! Small investment. LARGE RETURN. America's
#1 snack. Established micro route. CALL 1-800-

# 1 SNACK. $3,500 investment. Equipment included. 114%
Profit. CALL 1-800-
```

The popcorn phone pitch was:

"How would you like to become part of the billion dollar popcorn business? 99 out of 100 people eat popcorn and we are offering you an opportunity to become part of this industry for only $3,500. That includes Litton state-of-the-art microwave equipment and enough product to almost double your investment. We have people who are contacting prime tavern locations in your area right now. If you're interested in this type of program, we'll overnight you a C.O.D. package of information."

I kept it brief. I didn't tell the mooch how much popcorn he would be receiving or the size of the microwave. Nor did I explain about the locating fee. Only give the mooch information if he insists. Push the C.O.D., Fed-Ex package.

First page of the marketing pamphlet:

I would like to thank you for inquiring into this unique business opportunity.

Nearly everyone I speak with has considered going into business. However, for various reasons, they continue working for their present employer and have not taken any serious steps to enhance their present financial status.

The proposal offered by POP LIGHT gives that person a chance to become financially independent without great financial risk (only $3,500). Due to our expertise and the popularity of the product, the success of POP LIGHT is one of the highest in the country. The cost is low, the profit on popcorn is high.

WHICH SNACK IS WHOLESOME, NATURAL, ECONOMICAL, DELICIOUS AND FUN? — POPCORN!!! 630 Million pounds are sold annually — 42 quarts for every man, woman and child. Popcorn sales double every 10 years. It's the world's number one-selling, most profitable snack food.

With our state-of-the-art micro-poppers, all you do is go to the location, drop off a case of popcorn and collect your money. What could be simpler? No employees, no risk. Work out of your house. Attain financial security. Your locations will be the best. Professional locators will make sure of that.

Read over our material. You will be amazed at the profit in popcorn. In a good grossing tavern you can sell 20 portions a day. That translates into a profit of $7,300 a year FOR JUST ONE LOCATION !

I will contact you later this week with information on other successful distributors.

Profit On Popcorn Project

COST OF POPCORN PROJECT
(10 units per sale.)

Microwaves @ $30 ea. (government auction): $30 x 10 = $ 300.00
Popcorn (100 cases per 10 displays) $6.50/case x 100 =   650.00
Copies of marketing pamphlet: =   30.00
Singer fee: $20 a unit x 10 = $200 x 2 singers =   400.00

1-800-number:	75.00
(lots of calls on $3,500 ads)	
Business line (lots of return calls):	175.00
Answering service (above average use):	85.00
Newspaper ad:	175.00
Locating expenses — gas, food, motel, etc.:	250.00
	——————
Total Costs:	$2,140.00

Money Taken In On Popcorn Project:

10 Microwaves x $350 =	3,500.00
100 Cases popcorn x $12.96/case =	1,296.00
Distributing fee =	300.00
right to use POP LIGHT name (On a lower priced project, try squeezing the mooch for the right to distribute your product. It helps cover the singers and extra phone bills.)	
Locating fee $100/unit x 10 =	1,000.00
Total:	$6,096.00
Cost of Product:	$2,140.00
	——————
PROFIT:	$3,956.00

(I sold and located 10 of these packages in 90 days. My net profit — $39,560.)

If you are interested in doing a project of this nature, you'll need to contact a restaurant supply company or a name-brand microwave distributor. Get a price on 10 to 50 .5-cu. ft. microwave units. Have the store give you a picture of the unit, then contact Deli Express, 1-800-328-8184, and get a popcorn price. (You might be able to get the same or a better price from a local distributor.) After you have all that info, run your ad and wait for the phone to ring.

Locating

The best places for these units are bars. Call on the bar owner either early in the morning, 8-9, or in the middle of the afternoon. Since the microwaves are light, carry one in and ask the bar owner if you can pop some corn for his patrons. Tell him you are not selling it, but if he likes the popcorn, you will leave him a microwave and a case of popcorn at no cost. Explain that he only pays for what sells and he will be netting $30 a case. Selling price for a bag of popcorn: $1.25.

Most taverns like having hot popcorn; it enhances their booze sales.

The idea behind a popcorn route is easy to understand. I purchase the popcorn for $6.50 a case. I sell it to the mooch for $12.95 a case. He in turn sells it to the tavern for $31.20. There are 48 bags of popcorn. The tavern gets $1.25 a bag. This means the tavern will be getting $60 for the popped product.

This is another "sell then buy" program. Even if you only sell one package of 10 microwaves, there is still a lot of profit in it and you will know how to biz-op another product.

Chapter 18:
Pay Phones

◆ ◆ ◆ ◆ ◆ ◆ ◆ ◆ ◆

The most economical way to biz-op pay phones is with used equipment. Running an ad in the classifieds can pay dividends. "LOOKING FOR USED PAY PHONES. WILL PAY CASH. CALL #" You will be surprised how many people have purchased new pay phones but are unable to place them. The most you want to pay is $300.

Most phone companies have an annual used equipment auction. (Call and ask.) Included in the auction will be used pay phones. If you do not want to mess with an auction, call the big as well as smaller phone companies and inquire about used pay phones. Explain that you are going to convert them into lamps. It is usually much easier to work with the smaller, independent phone companies. Regardless, your best buys are still at the big phone company auctions. I have picked up good-looking, salable, older phones for as low as $25 a unit.

Some of the pay phones might be inoperable, but they can be made to look good. (It's a rare mooch who knows the innards of a pay phone.) You want phones that a professional appliance repair man can polish into new looking units. (I have mine done by a professional company that does appliance painting and repair. Cost $75 a unit. You can do it yourself for a couple cans of paint, spit, polish and elbow grease.) How do you sell a good-looking phone that doesn't work? Simple: the phones are never installed because there is no place to put them.

Next time you're driving around, stop in a convenience store and ask the manager if he signed a contract for his pay phone. The answer, even though he may not know the terms of the agreement, is always yes. The contract runs from 5 to 10 years. They are legally binding and not worth the legal expense of trying to break. Even if the store owner sells the store, the contract is considered part of the sale and is passed on.

Most store owners couldn't care less about their pay phone contract and a new owner may be unaware of it. You, as the locator (or a locating company) can get an unaware store owner to sign a new contract for a mooch's pay phone. (See the Appendix for pay phone contract.) The main pitch is you will pay him twice the amount that his present phone company is paying. (10 percent is standard.) Plus you will pay a $50 cash sign up bonus when the phone is installed. Since the contract with the old phone company cannot be broken, you do not have to worry about actually paying the cash bonus. All you want is a high traffic location to sign a contract so you can collect your locating fee. Locating pay phones by using the $50 bonus, higher percentage pitch is easy. It also pays well. I charge $300 a unit, half up front, the other half on completion.

This is one time you let a mooch take his time when he tours his locations. Stroll in with the mooch. Introduce him as the town's newest phone company owner. Let the mooch and owner chat while you use a measuring tape to get the dimensions of the old phone display (all a smoke screen). If the owner of the store happens to mention the $50, tell the mooch that's part of your program and you will take care of it.

After the mooch has completed his tour, you explain that the first thing he must do is contact the old phone company and have the old pay phone removed. Then he has to get in touch with an independent phone installer and make arrangements to have his pay phone installed. The last step is to have his new number activated.

Aftermath

Expect a call from your phone mooch within seven days. He will be very upset because the existing phone contracts cannot be broken. He will want to know what you are going to do. If you have several other phone deals in the works, you will not be able to close up shop and disappear. So, your job over the next few weeks will be to provide an encouraging voice. "That's impossible," you tell the mooch. "I've put almost 50 of those phones in locations exactly like the ones you have. I'll get my attorney on this right away. I know we can straighten this out. Just give my attorney time to work on it." Stall the mooch for a few weeks with attorney excuses. "He's out of town." "He's in court." When the mooch again reaches the boiling point, spring the good news on him. "My attorney has reached an agreement with the existing phone company and they are going to remove their phones. It cost me a grand to work all this out, but I intend to get you set up and making money."

By this time, you should be ready to change your 1-800-number and go on vacation.

*Used pay phones, such as this, are cheaper,
and, therefore, more profitable to the biz-opper.*

Profit On Pay Phone Project

Cost Of Pay Phone Project

The cost of a pay phone project depends on how much you pay for the phones. The most I have ever paid is $150, so we will use that as the "high end price." You should always try to sell a package of three, but if a mooch only wants one, then make him happy by sticking it to him for $2,500. (If you want to go with new pay phones, they can be purchased at Alltel Supply Inc., 6625 The Corners Pkwy., Waycross, GA 30092. 1-800-533-3161. QURDUM pay phones will cost you $960, AT&T $1,100. I have never purchased new units. I only do pay phone projects once every three years — too much heat.)

Three pay phones $150 x 3 =	$ 450.00
Cost of refurbishing $75 x 3 =	225.00
Boxes for pay phones: $25 ea. x 3 =	75.00
(You want excellent ones stamped "Telephone.")	
Singer fee: $50 a unit x 3 = $150 x 2 singers =	300.00
(only to be paid if deal closes)	
1-800-number starter-line (incoming calls):	30.00
Business line return calls:	75.00
Answering service:	45.00
Newspaper ad (per week):	150.00
Locating expenses — gas, food, motel, etc.:	250.00
Copies of marketing pamphlet:	30.00
	_____
Total Costs:	$1,630.00

Pay Phone Project Profit

A standard price for one pay phone is $2,500, but most packages consist of three pay phones. For three pay phones, the price is $2,000 each. For six, it's $1,500 each. Never go any lower than $1,500 unless the mooch wants to do something really stupid such as buying 20; then we bottom out at $1,000 each. We will use the standard three-pack in this example:

Three pay phones @ $2,000 ea. =	$6,000.00
Locating fee - $300/unit =	900.00
(I am setting this up as just one sale, but in a major city,	
you should be able to move at least nine pay phones.)	
Total:	$6,900.00
Cost:	$1,630.00
	_____
PROFIT:	$5,270.00

Newspaper Ads

ALL CASH BUSINESS. Pay phone route being established in your area. Fantastic return. 1-800-

PAY PHONES. GREAT LOCATIONS AVAILABLE LOCALLY. AT&T, MCI, ETC. 1-800-

$ PAY TELEPHONES $ Pre-installation income verification. Full training. Professionally selected locations. From $6,000. 1-800- 24 hours.

(Using the AT&T and MCI names means nothing. All phones will take either one. It just sounds more impressive.)

Pre-installation income is the pay sheet the store owner receives each month. It shows how much the phone is grossing and what the owner's share is. If you ask the store owner about it, he will probably give it to you, especially if you are offering to double his percentage plus give him a $50 sign up bonus. (See REFERENCE chapter.)

Pay Phone Project Phone Pitch

"How would you like to be part of the $10 billion U.S. pay phone business? (Sounds interesting.) Well, what we are offering is a unique opportunity to join this industry. In your area we have on-site, full time locators who are securing prime locations, locations that are guaranteed to return your investment in six months."

At this time you have kicked in the greed factor: You've told him it's a $10 billion industry and he's going to get a quick financial response. You can go on explaining about the quality of the pay phone, but you have to set the hook, and do not need to carry on an in-depth conversation. You want him to accept the Fed-Ex package. If he doesn't, don't waste your time. Go on to your next call.

Marketing Pamphlet

Hello_____

Welcome to the age of communications. On a daily basis, everyone touches a communication tool — T.V., radio, fax, phone, etc. It is the largest business in the world. Giants such as AT&T, US West and MCI control billions. Pay telephones generate over $10 billion yearly in the U.S. Approximately 25 billion $.25 pay phone calls are placed annually in this country. That figure does not include credit card calls which are almost equal to coin drop revenues.

The pay phone business growth factor will never stop. The demand for pay phones in commercial businesses is increasing. You can become part of this phenomenal growth through DYNAMIC PAY PHONES OF AMERICA.

We are offering you high-traffic locations that will start making you money on the first day. Each phone will only require 15 minutes of your time weekly. You can operate out of your own house. The work is light and pleasant. You have no employees, no wages, no employee taxes. This is among the least labor intensive of businesses available for investment today.

Our trouble-free automated phones eliminate all down time. Like silent salesmen, they stand quietly earning you money. They do not get sick. They work day and night. Telephones are not affected by economic recession. It requires no skill or special training. Telephones simply sell voice service, leaving you, the owner, to enjoy your free time as you like. Our pay phones have been accumulating profits for our operators at an ever increasing rate. You will be able to talk to other financially secure operators, who, like yourself, wanted something better out of life — a chance to become independent and financially secure. They have done this with DYNAMIC PAY PHONES OF AMERICA, so can you.

Read over our material. I am sure you will agree — THIS IS A ONCE IN A LIFETIME OPPORTUNITY. I will be calling back in a few days. At that time I will put you in touch with some of our financially secure operators.

Chapter 19: Pay Fax

◆ ◆ ◆ ◆ ◆ ◆ ◆ ◆ ◆

At present, pay faxes are the biggest biz-op rip off. They are also more in tune to a biz-opper who has money. A mooch is charged from $4,000 to $7,000 a unit. In order for a biz-opper to get a wholesale price of $1,200, he must purchase 50 units. There are very few used ones.

A pay fax is nothing more than a glorified phone with a built-in fax and a credit card strip. It will not take coins, only credit cards. A primary pay fax pitch is: The pay fax will produce from 10 to 20 transactions a day. The average transmission is three pages, the charge, $12; 10 transactions, $120, 20 transactions, $240. The mooch is assured this will happen because of his guaranteed locations, locations such as county court houses, the airport, train stations, Red Lions and Holiday Inns. All high traffic fax places.

One of the nice things about a mooch is they never do any location research. A good mooch always believes what a biz-opper tells him. Most of the time they are blinded by greed. If they were to do a little research, they would discover airports have their own public pay fax systems, major hotels do not intend to give up their lucrative fax money, and court houses have a fax in every office.

In order to locate a public fax system, you have to revert to malls, photo centers, smaller motels and convenience stores. You sell the mooch on this by telling him you have other customers who only have those types of locations and they are getting rich.

Since most people have never seen a public fax, it makes them easy to locate. Try to find a location that has a public copier. Copiers and pay faxes go hand in hand. Once you tell a store owner you are going to give him a free fax system, he will listen. The mooch pays for the phone line and the installation. The location provides the space and gets 15 percent for doing that.

Part of the fax pitch is: The biz-opper's main office will handle all the mooch's fax credit card billing. When someone uses a credit card on the mooch's pay fax, the billing will go through the biz-op operator's main office. They in turn will take 16 percent for processing the paper work and sending the mooch his check. (This is done by having the swipe temporarily hooked up to an established credit card billing company, not the biz-op office.)

To the mooch this sounds like the easy life. Kick back, lie in the sun, belt down expensive wine and get a fat monthly fax check. Unfortunately, the mooch will not be able to buy a glass of beer with his fax check. The major problem with the pay fax is the way fax users respond to them. Even though the fax works, nobody will use it. People are afraid to swipe their credit card through for fear of someone getting their card number. People are also lazy. Why go through all the trouble of reading fax sending instructions when you can go to a Mail Box Etc. and send a cheaper, hassle-free fax?

Now comes the cute part. If no one is sending faxes, there is no need to keep up the credit card billing system. After the last pay fax has been sold, the credit card billing system is discontinued and the operation is shut down.

I will include some information on purchasing pay faxes, but if you are a beginner, I suggest you stay away from this program. A pay fax biz-opper is well seasoned and he has the money to back a pay fax project.

There are two ways to purchase pay faxes. The most economical way is to run an ad in several major newspapers. It should read "LOOKING FOR USED PAY FAXES. WILL PAY CASH FOR FAXES IN GOOD CONDITION 1-800-." Do not pay any more than $500 a unit. You may not get a single call, pay faxes are still rare.

Pay faxes can be purchased at Comtel Data Systems, Inc., East Dundee, IL. 708-426-0077. In order to get a wholesale price, you must purchase 50 units at $1,200 each.

Pay Fax Profit

The entire cost of a new pay fax package, including telephone, 1-800 number, cost of pay fax, singers, etc., is $4,350. You will sell and locate the package for $15,000. Your net profit on a new pay fax deal will be $10,800, but remember, if you do not find used faxes, you will have to spend $60,000 up front purchasing new ones.

Ads

A typical pay fax ad reads like this:

```
OUTSTANDING OPPORTUNITY. Public fax machines. Credit card
activated. In excellent locations. Phenomenal return on
investment. $15K will secure your future. 1-800-.
```

A pay fax is nothing more than a glorified phone
with a built-in fax and a credit card strip.

Chapter 20: Doing Business With Other Biz-Oppers

◆ ◆ ◆ ◆ ◆ ◆ ◆ ◆ ◆

Throughout the United States there are numerous biz-op locating companies. (See REFERENCE chapter.) They all sell and locate products of their own as well as products for other biz-op operators. If you do a locating job for another biz-opper, always find out who is paying, the biz-opper or the mooch. Preferably it will be the mooch. He has cash. The other biz-opper might have a questionable check.

Small biz-op operators do a lot of their own locating, but many of them devote as much as 50 percent of their time locating other operators' products. If a small operator hits on a hot product, he will switch from local papers to *USA Today*. Because of his size he will be unable to take on a national locating program. Instead, he will concentrate on selling and let other biz-operators handle the locating work. He only releases this work after a locating fee has been established. Out of that fee, he is to receive a 10 percent kickback. If he doesn't, he will drop that locating company and go to another one.

I exchange work with a lot of biz-op operators. If I sell a mooch 10 vending machines in Texas, I will not make a trip to locate them. Instead I contact two biz-op operators in that part of the country and tell them about the mooch. I then give the mooch the phone numbers of the two operators. The mooch can then decide whom he wants to work with. The same is true for the Pacific Northwest. If a Texas biz-opper is selling a package in Portland, he will contact me. (For the benefit of all new biz-op operators, NEVER SELL PRODUCTS IN YOUR HOME STATE. Some biz-op marketers in larger states get away with this, but they have to set up a confusing system of dummy companies and off-brand 800 numbers. It is also much easier to get lost in a heavily populated area.)

It's all right to locate in your own state. Locating is considered a service. As long as you provide the mooch with legal, signed locating agreements and he signs the acceptance form (see the Appendix), you have fulfilled your contract.

When you are contacted by another biz-opper's mooch, let him know that you are a local, not an out-of-state, locator. A mooch wants somebody who is familiar with his city.

Tell him you have customers with vending machines (for example) similar to his that are doing extremely well — as a matter of fact, they are doing so well they have expanded from 10 to 30 vending machines. Make it clear that you have the same vending machine in stock at a lower price. If he is buying them for $700, tell him you you can get them for him for $500. Explain that 50 percent of your business is repeat business. "My established customers are my bread and butter," is the phrase I use over and over. You want the "mooch" to understand that his machines are going to make good money and you would like to become part of his expansion program: "If you work with me, I will make sure that all of your locations are profitable."

The last thing you tell the mooch is, "I will be sending you a contract. Please sign and return it along with a cashier's check for half of the locating fee." The other half will be collected when the job is finished.

When doing smaller jobs for other biz-oppers, do not kickback 10 percent. The same is true when they are doing a small job for you. The "paying point" is $5,000 and above.

Post Script

◆ ◆ ◆ ◆ ◆ ◆ ◆ ◆ ◆

This book contains a few of the things I have offered through biz-op marketing. There are many others, but describing everything is repetitious. The system is always the same. Find a product, revamp your marketing pamphlet, run newspaper ads, get mooch's money, buy product and locate. If you follow these steps and have no qualms about screwing people, you should find the biz-op racket to your liking. GOOD LUCK.

References

♦ ♦ ♦ ♦ ♦ ♦ ♦ ♦ ♦

Biz-Op Locating Companies

This list was put together on April 10, 1993. Some of these companies stay in business for quite some time; others only operate for a few months. I know most of these biz-oppers. If they get another 1-800 number, they usually contact me. I suggest you make calls to all of them and explain that you will be marketing products and might have some locating work for them. (Even if you are going to do it yourself, it pays to touch base with these people.) Let them know you will be available to help if they need locating in your area. Bullshit them. Don't tell them you're a novice. You can make a lot of money off doing other biz-oppers' locating jobs. DON'T TELL THEM YOU FOUND THEIR NAME IN A BOOK. Remember you're dealing with a pack of wolves.

When you talk to the different locating companies, tell them you are looking for used vending machines. Some of the companies will have re-buy vends. Just make sure they will send them C.O.D. If not, you had better drive down and check them out.

North American Vending Corp.
3400 NE 12th Ave, Suite 179
Oakland Park, FL 3334
Business phone 305-568-9420
RobertD. Sparks, President
Vitamin Vending

Prime Time Locating
28870 U.S. Hwy. 1 North, Suite 300
Clearwater, FL 34621
813-726-4167
Dave Evans

World Wide
22941 Triton Way, Suite 241
Laguna Hills, CA 92654
1-800-444-4172
Business phone 714-588-0874
Ron Johnson, Ken Marshall

American Locators, Inc.
2814 Spring Rd., Suite 116
Atlanta, GA 30339
1-800-843-5580
Jim Whitter

J and L
303 Third St. N.E.
Arab, AL 35016
1-800-325-7887
Business phone 205-586-7887
Laura and John Higgins

Excell
612 Bain Dr.
Huntsville, AL 35803
1-800-688-9100
Business phone 205-880-9052
Ed

The above biz-oppers have been around for a year. The biz-oppers on the following list have had their 1-800 numbers for about six months.

Universal Vendor
1610 South La Cienega Blvd Suite 205
Los Angeles, CA 90035
1-800-877-7987

Phoenix Locating
2310 State Rd. #5411
Lutez, FL 33549
1-800-487-1006
Phil Daily

Challenger Marketing
2235 N. Courtenay
Parkway, FL 32953
1-800-749-9177
Stan Hodges

U.S.A. Locating
2503 Canyon Ridge Ct.
Arlington, TX 76006-4001
1-800-572-1223
Dale Hittion

Quality Vending
1905 Sherman St., Suite 300
Denver, CO 80203
1-800-568-2134
Jay Levine, owner
    Jay sells all his vending machines with
    the location fee included in the price.

U.S. Marketing
1-800-638-1342
Marty

Redskin Locating Service
Missouri
314-965-6173
S. Crissman

Four Star Professional Locating
Dallas, TX
1-800-677-5577
Sherie

Gemini Marketing
Huntsville, AL
1-800-873-6094
Business phone 205-882-2881
Jim Christensen

Rosenthal Locating
Las Vegas, NV
1-800-821-6029
Rosenthal

Coin Tex
Kentucky
615-943-4702
Danny Woodward

United Locations
6659 Peachtree Industrial Blvd.
  Suite F
Atlanta, GA 30092
1-800-416-9688
Steve Moneyham, owner

Quality Locations
600 N. Winebach, Suite 250
Evansville, IN 47711
1-800-879-9239
Gordon

All American Locating
707 N. Main, Suite B
Evansville, IN 47711
1-800-477-8087
Clif Rednour
　　Clif is the brother of Ted Rednour. Ted owns
　　North American Locating.

Paramount Promotions
1-800-964-8737

Jimco and Associates
7737 Fair Oaks Blvd Suite 480
Carmichael, CA 95608-1792
916-944-2359
Jim McVicar

Merit Industries
2525 State Road
Bensalem, PA 19020
1-800-523-2760
　　Video Poker

Telecomm Inc.
Plaza 322 Route 46
West Parsippany, NJ 07054
1-800-232-9824
　　Pay faxes

National Tech Services
3345 W. Hospital Ave.
Atlanta, GA 30341
1-800-638-1342
Jack

Morgan-Ashley
Denver, CO
1-800-234-3346
Joe Degeudul

Dave Slaughter
1-800-376-6474

USA Locating
Dallas, TX
1-800-572-1223
Maurice Billion

Drew's Distribution Inc.
PO Box 632
Fairforest, SC 29336
803-574-0163
　　Crane machines.

Greyhound's Skill Cranes
Rt 37 & Germania Rd
PO Box 1697
Toms River, NJ 08754
1-800-222-0491
　　Crane machines

Vending Machine Manufacturers
Prices current as of April 20, 1993

Edina Technical Products
1925 Annapolis Ln.
Plymouth, MN 55441
612-557-8000
　　Edina has the standard mechanical vend. They manufacture the counter tops 22"
high x 30" wide x 19" deep, weight 90 lbs. You can get 50 of these for $270 each or a

hundred at $200 each. The retail depends upon the mooch. I've sold C.T.s as high as $800 each and as low as $350 each. The average price is $600 each. (See picture.) Edina also carries the upright vends (floor models). These vends are 55" high x 28" wide x 21" deep, weight 140 lbs. The upright vend is basically two counter tops stacked on each other and put into a metal box. Fifty of these will cost $600 each, 100 units $500 each. Retail $2,000-$2,500 each or whatever the market will bear.

Edina also stocks microwave snack machines 55" high x 28" wide x 21" deep, weight 157 lbs. The microwave uses 110-120-15 amp; U.L. approved. It is shipped separately. Fifty units, $700 each: 100 units, $600 each. Retail $2,500-$3,500 each.

Mechanical Countertop Vending Machine available from
Edina Technical Products.

American Futuro Corp.
P.O. Box 606
369 Garden Ct.
Grove City, OH 43123
614-875-9207

American Futuro carries the combination postage stamp, sticker, laminating vends. These are your most common stamp-type of machines. Kids like them because they have stickers of their favorite cartoon characters, rock stars or sports heroes. The machines also will laminate pictures or I.D.s and dispense stamps and envelopes. Height is 21", width 12", depth 8", weight 35 lbs. If you become a distributor, you can purchase the vends for $199 each. Retail $599. In order to become a distributor, you need to purchase 50 machines.

LeBron Mfg.
LeBron Bldg.
1492 S. 1 6th St.
Omaha, NE
402-342-21 76

    LeBron manufactures the hot soup, microwave-type of vending machine 55" high x 28" wide x 21" deep, weight 175 lbs. It pops popcorn, spits out hot soups, heats breakfast rolls and has a selection of chips and candy. Cost for 5 units, $800 each. Retail $2,500. (See picture.)

Floor Model, Microwave Vending Machine
Available from LeBron Mfg.

Vend-Rite Manufacturing Company
1750 W. North Ave.
Chicago, IL 60622
312-772-6700

Vend-Rite manufactures compact candy and cigarette vending machines. Their slickest machine is the Ferrara Pan Candy Store. It is 5" deep, 24" high and 18" wide: weight 26 lbs. It holds 25-cent boxes of the candy kids love most — Red Hots, Lemon Drops, etc. It will either mount on a wall or has a pedestal. Your cost, $350. It retails for $750.

Vend-Rite's cigarette, candy machine is 18" wide x 11 " deep x 24½" high: weight 95 lbs. These units also sell for $350, but they retail for $795.

Seaga Corporation
401 W. Arch
Shannon, IL 61078
815-864-2600

Seaga carries three basic vending machines. One is the Super Vend 2000, a dual-headed bulk candy dispenser. It sits on a pedestal. Its height is 46", depth 8", width 13"; weight 24 lbs. Your cost on 20 of these units is $89 each. Retail $250. Seaga also handles the C.T.s. They are the same basic size as Edina's C.T.s. Your cost on 20 to 50 vends is $250 each. Over 50, they drop to $200 each. They will retail for as high as $800. Seaga's floor model vends are the same size as Edina's. Your cost, $450 each for 10. Retail, up to $2,100. Seaga is an easy company to work with.

Other American Vending Companies

Vendo
7209 N. Ingran Ave.
Fresno, CA 93650
209-431-1770
Candy vends.

Shipman Mfg.
13265 Lorena St.
Los Angeles, CA 90023
213-261-6151
Soda, candy vends.

Auto Photo Systems
2722 Walnut Ave.
Tustin, CA 92680
714-731-3121
Photo and self-serve business cards.

Robo Vend
4694 E. 10th Ct.
Hialeah, FL 33013
305-688-4994
Popcorn vends.

Eagle Vending Machines
1640 Powers Ferry, Bldg. 21
Atlanta, GA 30067
404-590-0986
Candy, soda.

Leskro Vends
911 Sullivan Rd.
Aurora, IL 60506
708-896-8555
Snack, candy.

Reliable Engineering
1537 N. Lockwood Ave.
Chicago, IL 60651
313-735-5113
    Sanitary napkins, condoms,
    ball-point pens, postage stamps.

Fawn Engineering
P.O. Box 1333
Des Moines, IA 50305
515-274-3641
    Candy, soda.

Gross-Given
75 W. Plato Blvd.
St. Paul, MN 55107
612-224-4391
    Candy, cigarettes, pastry, snack, coffee.

Ford Gum and Machine Company
Hoad and Newton Ave.
Akron, NY 14001
716-542-4561
    Snack vending and ball gum machines.

Postage Stamp Machine Company
2008-12 Utica Ave.
Brooklyn, NY 11234
718-241-8500

Target Manufacturing Ltd.
Suite 201 17919 Roan Place
Cloverdale, BC Canada V3S 5K1
604-576-1322
    Popcorn vend.

North Western Corp.
Morris, IL 60450
815-942-1300
    Vitamin capsules, ball gum.

Victor Vending
900 Parker Ave.
Dassel, MN 55325
612-275-2121
    Vitamin capsules, candy, bulk
    gum.

Roe International
75 N. Bellview Rd.
Whippany, NJ 07981
201-887-0400
    Coffee, cigarettes, soda.

Cavalier Corp.
1105 E. 10th
Chattanooga, TN 37403
615-267-6671
    Vending machines, can soda.

National Vending Systems Inc.
1440 Kennedy Causeway,
  Suite 1424
North Bay Village, FL 33141
1-800-736-8363
    Candy vending.

North American Vending
Denver, CO
    Jerry Golden

    As you can see, there is a large selection of vending companies to choose from. I suggest that you either write or call the companies and request pictures and prices. Tell them you're a business opportunity marketer and you're going to be putting together an ad campaign for C.T. vends and you want the best deal you can get. Explain that you just finished "offing" 200 seed displays and you are looking to start a new project. Don't let them think you're an amateur.

    One of the drawbacks to new, state-of-the-art vends is you cannot triple your price. Like all new items, it takes awhile for the price to drop. The Ferrara Pan Candy Store that Vend-Rite has is a nice unit, but you will not be able to triple your price. It's better to stay with a company that has a large stock of C.T.s.

If you use the "sell then buy" method, you need to know the price of your vends before you start quoting prices to the mooch. Remember, you should triple the wholesale price of the vend. If you're paying $200 for a new vend, you sell it for $600. If it's a $100 used vend, you still sell it for $600. Obviously, it's more profitable to track down used vending machines.

Do not be afraid to tell the vending machine rep that you got a better price from another vending machine company. He just might come back with a lower price. Always ask if they have used machines in stock. Sometimes they will. It's your job to look out for yourself. PROFIT IS THE NAME OF THE GAME.

Box Manufacturers

The following is a list of places where charity honor boxes can be purchased. If the companies are not local, they can put you in touch with one that is. This is also the list sent out in the "Assemble Your Own Charity Honor Box" project.

United States Box Corp.
1294 McCarter Hwy
Newark, NJ 07104
201-481-3000
or 718-387-1510

General Box Company
Dept. 50
710 Haines Ave.
Waycross, GA
912-283-5716

Mac Chicago Corporation
2445 S. Rockwell, Dept. 17
Chicago, IL 60608
1-800-992-6225, Ext. 17

House of Cardboard
3524 W. Potomac
Chicago, IL 60651
312-342-3600, Ext. 26

Stock Boxes
P.O. Box 14015
Dayton, OH 45413-0015
513-898-1700

Corrulite
P.O. Box 2307
Clewiston, FL 33440
407-996-2089

Capitol Containers
123-A N. Des Plains St.
Chicago, IL 60606
312-454-1515

Fleetwood Containers
2721 E. 45th St.
Los Angeles, CA 90058
213-588-7121

Packing Company of California
6400 E. Washington Blvd.
P.O. Box 91-1191
Los Angeles, CA 90040
213-722-4330

Crocket Containers
9211 Norwalk Blvd.
Santa Fe Springs, CA 90670
310-692-9455

International Packing
337 N. Cascade, Dept. T
Colorado Springs, CO 80907
1-800-821-1633

Kiva Containers
2830 W. Osborn Rd.
Phoenix, AZ 85017
602-258-8383

A.1. Halper Corrugated Box Co.
900 6th Ave. S.E.
Minneapolis, MN 55414
1-800-959-0989

E-Z Pack
6545 Wiehe Rd.
Cincinnati, OH 45237
1-800-895-1351

Westvaco Container Company
P.O. Box 29411-05
New Charleston, SC 29411
1-800-745-3066

Accurate Corrugated Boxes
7350 Stiles Dr.
El Paso, TX 79915-2552
915-778-7350

Inland Container Corp.
Corporate Headquarters
4030 Vincennes Rd.
Indianapolis, IN 46268-0937
317-879-4222
    Sales Offices:
    Newark, CA 415-790-7440
    Stamford, CT (New York) 203-324-9277
    Chicago, IL 312-562-6100
    Indianapolis, IN 317-879-4430
    St. Louis, MO 612-445-4201
    Dallas,   TX 214-380-5511

Brookfield Box Co.
3269 Ettie St.
Oakland, CA 94608
510-653-0522

Mason Box Company
521 Mt. Hope St.
North Attlboro, ME 02761-6129
1-800-225-2708

Argos Box Company
P.O. Box 14015
Dayton, OH 45413-0015
513-898-1700

Mefo
Walnut and Center St.
North Wales, PA 19454
215-699-8755

International Containers
6400 Poplar Ave.
Memphis, TN 38119
1-800-223-1266

Jim Dandy Boxes
1505 Royal Parkway
Euless, TX 76040
817-540-1444

Apple Corrugated Packing
4433 Bronze Way
Dallas, TX 75236-2005
214-331-9000

Corrugated Box Plants:

Fort Smith, AR	501-785-4211	Buena Park, CA	714-670-7603
El Centro, CA	619-353-9906	Los Angeles, CA	213-724-5010
Newark, CA	415-797-2020	Ontario, CA	213-724-5010
Santa Fe Springs, CA	213-692-9465	Tracy, CA	209-836-1971
Wheat Ridge, CO	303-422-7700	Orlando, FL	407-855-2121
Macon, GA	912-788-4500	Rome, GA	404-232-1525
Chicago, IL	312-562-6100	Crawfordsville, IN	317-362-4010
Evansville, IN	812-429-0389	Indianapolis, IN	317-634-4441
Garden City, KS	316-276-6349	Kansas City, KS	913-321-1414
Louisville, KY	502-459-8800	Minden, LA	318-371-1414
Minneapolis, MN	612-445-4201	Hattiesburg, MS	601-544-7400
St. Louis, MO	314-225-4900	Edison, NJ	201-548-3400
Spotswood, NJ	201-251-2000	Middletown, OH	513-425-0830
Biglerville, PA	717-677-8121	Erie, PA	814-455-9031
Hazleton, PA	717-384-3251	Vega Alta, PR	809-721-3434
Lexington, SC	803-359-5101	Rock Hill, SC	803-366-4103
Elizabethton, TN	615-542-2112	Knoxville, TN	615-525-5703
Dallas, TX	214-416-2691	Edinburg, TX	512-383-4939
Richmond, VA	804-231-1137		

Plastic Companies

These are plastic companies that carry material for the Jackpots. If they are not local, they will be able to direct you to someone in your area. This is also the list that is sent out in the voice mail "Assemble Your Own Honor Boxes and Jackpots" project.

New Age Industries
2300-21 Maryland Rd.
Willow Grove, PA 19090-1799
215-657-3151

Ono Industries
P.O. Box 150
Ono, PA 17077
717-863-6919

Universal Plastic
4200 Jackson St.
Denver, CO 80216
1-800-395-8706

Resdel Corporation
P.O. Box 3952
Greenville, DE 19807-3952
1-800-437-1062

IMPLEX
1685 S. Mt. Prospect Rd.
Des Plains, IL 60018
708-827-7049

Tulox
Dept. 6, Miller Ave.
Marion, IN 46952
317-664-5155
Free catalog.

Petro Plastic
650 South Ave.
Garland, NJ 07027
908-789-1200

Tri Lights Plastics
3901 Research Way
Corner Ave. Industrial Park
Pell City, AL 35125
1 -800-334-1395

Freelan-Wade
1730 Miller Ave.
P.O. Box 1007
McMinville, OR 97128
503-434-5561

World Plastics
150 W. Commercial Ave.
Moonachice, NJ 07073
201-933- 2915

Reham, Inc.
1800 Sierra Madre Circle, Dept. A
Placentia, CA 92670
714-666-0062

Professional Plastics
740 Monroe Way
Placentia, CA 92670
714-579-0755

Professional Plastics
4829 S. 36th St., #8
Phoenix, AZ 85040
602-437-4555

Term Plastics
1268 Valley Rd.
Shirling, NJ 07980
908-561-3000

Organ Plastics
P.O. Box 299
Hubbard, OR 97032
503-981-1934

Sinclair & Rush
3545 Scarlet Oak Blvd.
St. Louis, MO
1-800-949-1141

Busada Louisa Industrial
Air Park
Louisa, VA 23092
707-967-2882

American Industrial Plastics
724 Fentress Blvd.
Daytona Beach, FL 32114
904-274-5335

Professional Plastics
55 Bonaventura Dr.
San Jose, CA 95134
408-433-1700

Pyramid Plastics
220 W. 5th St.
Hope, AR 71801
501-777-5759

Automotive Products

These companies can all be approached using a variation of the formatted letter in Chapter 16.

Waxes and Cleaners

Auto Wax Company
1300 Round Table Dr.
Dallas, TX 75247
214-631-4000
    Detergents, cleaners, polishes and waxes.

BKB Automotive Cosmetics
13400 Saticoy St.
North Hollywood, CA 91605
213-873-2065
    Waxes, polishes.

Hi-Luster
3512 Fowler St.
Los Angeles, CA 90063
213-269-3858
    Waxes, polishes.

High Luster
2945 Runus Rd.
Haywood, CA 94544
510-785-0196
    Waxes, polishes.

Mouthers Polishes
5456 Industrial Dr.
Huntington Beach, CA 92649
714-891-3364

Oscars
1691 California St.
Corona, CA 91719
1-800-959-1318
    Waxes, soap, detergent
cleaners.

S and S Car Care
5340 Mayfair Rd.
North Canton, OH 44720
216-494-9535
    Wax, polishes.

Additives for Oil and Gas

Automotive Accessories
241 41st St.
Brooklyn, NY 11322
718-499-3838

Bell Additives
1340 Bennett Dr.
Longwood, FL 32750
407-831-5021

Guardsman Products
411 N. Darling, Dept. SD
Freemont, MI 49412
1-800-766-8872

Champion Lubricants
605 Laguna Dr.
Richardson, TX 75080
1-800-880-3350

Imagineering Enterprise
1320 W. Sample
South Bend, IN 46619
1-800-723-4856

Kreen Motor Tonic
1079 R. Thompson Ln.
Nashville, TN 37211
615-833-4866

Lubricating Specialist
8015 Paramount Blvd.
Pico Rivera, CA 90660
310-928-3311

Lubrication Company of America
4212 E. Pacific Way
Los Angeles, CA 90023
213-264-1091

Lubrication Engineers
3851 Airport Freeway
Ft. Worth, TX
817-834-6321

QMI
360 Craftsman Blvd. #6B
Lakeland, FL 33803
1 -800-255-8138

Lubri-Loy Co.
6319 Wilson Ave.
St. Louis, MO 63139
314-654-6277

Lubricant Supply Company
75 Wisner Ave.
Middleton, NY 10940
914-343-4173

Octane Boost Corp.
222 Town E. Blvd.
Mesquite, TX 75149
214-289-0631

Toy Companies

These companies can all be approached using a variation of the formatted letter. (See Chapter 16.)

Creativity For Kids
1802 Central Ave.
Cleveland, OH 44115-2325
1-800-642-2288
   Toys that teach.

Chu's Magic International
#103-11860 Hammersmith Way
Richmond, B.C., V745GI, Canada
604-272-2700
   Magic tricks and games.

BRIO
6555 W. Mill Rd.
Milwaukee, WI 53218
1-800-558-6863
   Wooden toys.

Harmony Toys
570 Taxter Rd.
Elmsford, NY 10523
1-800-722-3263
   Cooperative play games.

Intex Recreation
P.O. Box 1440
4130 Sante Fe Ave.
Long Beach, CA 90801-1440
213-549-5400
   Die-cast toys and vinyl
   inflatables.

Steven Manufacturing
224 E. 4th St.
Hermann, MO 65041
314-486-5494
   Bedtime toys.

Gayla
6401 Antoine St.
P.O. Box 920800
Houston, TX 77292-0800
1-800-231-7508
  Kites, plastic and nylon.

Giggles Toy Co.
44854 Heydenreich Rd.
Mt. Clemens, MI 48044
313-468-4569
  Toys that glow in the dark.

Trophy Music Company
3800 Kelly Ave.
Cleveland, OH
1-800-321-0556
  Novelty instruments for children.

The Collectors Club
2707 McCone Ave.
Hayward, CA 84545
510-887-7168
  Stuffed animals.

Hope Industries
380 Smith St.
Farmingdale, NY 11735
516-777-8690
  Walt Disney products.

American-Made Country Critters
217 Neosho
Burlington, KS 66839
316-364-8623
  Plush, stuffed animals.

Anatomical Chart Co.
8221 Kiball Ave.
Skokie, IL 60076
1-800-621-7500
  Novelties, jewelry, puzzles.

Dgi-Buki
635 N.E. 4th Ave
Miami, FL 33138
305-751-3667
  Educational toys.

J. Kan
942 S. Long Beach Ave.
Los Angeles, CA 90021
213-623-7503
  Stuffed toys.

Poof Toy Products
4505 Helm St.
Plymouth, Ml 48170
313-454-9552.
  Assorted foam balls.

Bullyland, Inc.
36 W. 25th St.
NewYork, NY 10010
212-633-9575
  Assorted Betty Boop toys.

Toy Factory
1-800-257-1744
  Assortment of toys.

D & K Enterprises
218 Landing Court
Lee's Summit, MO 64064
816-478-1700
  Children's books.

Cosmetics Companies

The following is a list of cosmetics companies that you can send a variation of the formatted letter to. (See Chapter 16.)

Arizona Natural
2525 E. Beardsley
Phoenix, AZ 85024
602-569-6900

K.S.A. Joba
19023 Parthenia St.
Northridge, CA 91324
818-701-1534

Jolen Cream
25 Walls Dr.
Fairfield, CT 06430
203-259-8779

Key West Cosmetic Factory
P.O. Box 1079
Key West, FL 33041-1079
305-294-5592

Cosmyl
16115 N.W. 52nd Ave.
Miami, FL 33014
305-682-1112

N.D.G. Cosmetics
7601 Treasure Dr., Suite 1614
North Bay Village, FL 33141
305-861-8088

Erickson Cosmetics
1920 Clybour Ave.
Chicago, IL 60614
312-327-3800

Lanova Cosmetics
9326 Anthony Ave.
Chicago, IL 60617
312-375-5858

Ansell Benjamin
1555 Industrial Blvd.
St. Louis, MO 63132
314-429-4300

Gabriel Cosmetics
126 S. Ave. 18
Los Angeles, CA 90031
213-221-2430

Jafra Cosmetics
2451 Townsgate Rd.
Westlake Village, CA 91361
805-496-1911

Cascade International
2424 N. Federal Hwy., Suite 318
Boca Raton, FL 33431
407-338-8278.

Lady Godiva
7211 N.W. 35th St.
Miami, FL 33147-5833
305-696-6155

Miss Marion Cosmetics
1929 N.W. 20th St.
Miami, FL 33135-1641
305-325-0327

Creative Cosmetics
417 Richard Rd.
Rockledge, FL 32995
407-636-0717

Carson Products
P.O. Box 22309
Savanna, GA 31403
912-651-3400

Mineral Cosmetics
2824 Twelve Mile Rd.
Berkley, MI 48072
313-542-7733

Noyes P.J.
Box 381
Lancaster, NH 03584
603-788-4952

Paramount Cosmetics
135 38th St.
Union City, NJ 07087
201-865-8126

Dermac
Salem, OR
503-399-8181

Papelera Puetonigra
P.O. Box 40
Utnado, PR 00641
809-894-2098

Beauticontrol
3311 Boyington
Carrollton, TX 75006
214-458-0601

Textures
379 South West 13th Ave
Pompano Beach, FL 33069
305-946-0440

American Beauty Products
1623 E. Apache St.
Tulsa, OK 74106-4006
918-428-2577

Harmer
399 E. Baltimore Ave.
Landsdowne, PA 19050-2503
215-623-4462

Beauty Creations
1400 Regan
Memphis, TN 38101
901-774-9023

Panet Corp.
5700 W. Douglas Ave.
Milwaukee, WI 53218
414-462-0980

Card Companies

Gallent Greetings
2654 Medill Ave.
Chicago, IL 60647
312-489-2000

Sunshine Art Studio
45 Warwick St.
Springfield, MA 01101
431-781-5500

Thompson, Arthur and Company
4700 F. St.
Omaha, NE 68117
402-731-0411

Masterpiece Studio
5400 W. 35th St.
Cicero, IL 60650
707-656-4000

Hallmark Cards
P.O. Box 419580
Kansas City, MO 64141-6580
816-274-5111

American Greeting Cards
100500 American Rd.
Cleveland, OH 44144
216-252-7300

Paramount Card
400 Pine St.
P.O. Box 6465
Pawtucket, RI

Burgoyne, Inc.
2030 E. Bybery Rd.
Philadelphia, PA

Check your Yellow Pages for local greeting card companies. Tell them you are distributing toys to local stores and you want to add a cheap line of cards to your portfolio. For out of state card companies, use the formatted letter in Chapter 16.

Seed Companies

Petoseed Co., Inc.
1905 Lirio St.
Saticoy, CA 93004
805-647-1188

Crossman Seed Corp.
West Commercial and Crossman Terrace
P.O. Box 110
East Rochester, NY 14445
716-586-1928

Gurney Seed & Nursery
110 Capitol
Yankton, SD 57078
605-665-4451

N.K. Lawn and Garden Co.
7500 Olson Memorial Hwy.
Golden Valley, MN 55459
612-543-7236

Burpee Seeds
300 Park Ave.
Warminster, PA 18974
215-674-4900

International Specialty Supply
820 E. 20th
Cookeville, TN

Use a variation of the formatted letter in Chapter 16 when approaching the seed companies. The best time to run seed distributorship ads is during the winter. It gives the mooch a financial reason to look forward to spring.

```
BIG MONEY IN EXOTIC SEEDS. Limited distributorship. Only 6K
required. Call -
```

Overseas Markets

The following is a list of overseas markets. They will have a variety of merchandise. Write and ask what items they are closing out.

France, Belgium, Netherlands,
Italy and Spain
6 Ave. des Longs-Buts
14360 Trouville, France
Phone (33) 31 88 61 16

Japan
Nippon Service, Ltd.
3-9-5 Kotobuki
Taito-Ku, Tokyo, Japan
Phone (81) 3-3842-6001

Hong Kong
Sico Trading Company, Ltd.
Honytex Bldg., 10th Fl.
22 Ashley Rd.
Kowloon, Hong Kong
Phone (33) 852 376 1671

Taiwan
Trade Winds
P.O. Box 7-179
No. 7, Lane 75
Yung Kang St.
Taipei, Taiwan
Phone (88) 62 396-4022

Korea
World Marketing, Inc.
Dongbo Bldg.
81-9 Nohyun-Dong
Kangnam-Ku, Seoul,
135-010 Korea
Phone (82) 25 11 49 44

U.S. Government Auctions

General Services Administration
Regional Disposal Divisions

Region 1
Connecticut, New York, New Jersey, Massachusetts, Rhode Island, New Hampshire, Vermont and Maine.
John W. McCormack
Post Office and Courthouse
Boston, MA 02109
617-223-2651

Region 4
Delaware, Maryland, Virginia, West Virginia, Pennsylvania, North Carolina, Mississippi, South Carolina, Tennessee, Alabama, Georgia, Florida, Kentucky, National Capitol Area, Puerto Rico and the Virgin Islands.
75 Springs St. S.W.
Atlanta, GA 30303
404-221-5133

Region 5
Indiana, Illinois, Michigan, Wisconsin, Ohio and Minnesota.
230 Dearborn St.
Chicago, IL 60604
312-353-6064

Region 7
Kansas, Missouri, Iowa, Nebraska, Arkansas, Louisiana, New Mexico, Oklahoma and Texas.
819 Taylor St.
Fort Worth, TX 76102

Region 9
California, Nevada, Arizona, Hawaii, Guam, American Samoa and the trust territory of the Pacific Islands.
525 Market St.
San Francisco, CA 94105

Region 10
Alaska, Colorado, Idaho, Montana, North Dakota, Oregon, South Dakota, Utah, Washington and Wyoming.
GSA Center
Auburn, WA 98002
206-931-7548.

Any of these offices can either give you the time and place of government auctions or give you the number of a person who has that information.

Defense Reutilization And Marketing Regional Sales Offices

Defense Reutilization and Marketing
 Region Columbus
P.O. Box 500
Blacklick, OH 43003-0500
614-238-2114

Defense Reutilization and Marketing
Region Ogden
P.O. Box 53
Defense Depot
Ogden, UT 84407-5001
801-399-7257

Defense Reutilization and Marketing
Region Hawaii
Box 211
Pearl City, HI 96782-0211
808-455-5158

Defense Reutilization and Region
 Marketing
Region Memphis
P.O. Box 14716
Memphis, TN 38114-0716
901-775-6417

Defense Reutilization and
 Marketing
Region Europe
A.P.O. NY 09633
06121-82-3505

Defense Reutilization and Region
 Marketing
Region Australia
FPO San Francisco, CA 96680-2920
099-49-3214

National Sales Office D.O.D.
Bidders Control Office
P.O. Box 1370
Battle Creek, MI 49016-1370
616-962-6511, Ext. 6736

Glossary Of Biz-Op Slang

Back-up locations — extra locations for mooches' vending machines or displays.

Bagged a mooch — just screwed a customer.

Biz-opper — a person who runs business opportunity scam ads in a newspaper.

Biz-op tax shelter — an illegal tax operation.

Bon-bon eater — a housewife who is ripped off through work-at-home scams.

Cash and stash — cash checks: don't deposit them.

C.T. — counter top vending machines or displays.

Continuous runner — a newspaper ad that is successful.

Fly 'n' buy — when a biz-opper pays to fly a mooch to his company warehouse.

Give away — something you give a store owner to entice him to take your product.

Grabber — newspaper ad that makes false promises.

Greed factor — your product must appeal to the mooch's greed.

Guaranteed locations — locations that are guaranteed to make money or the displays will be moved.

Guaranteed sale — a store does not pay for a product until it is sold.

Header — sign that goes on top of display.

Hidden money — cash that is stashed for tax reasons.

Hit and run money — money that is taken from a mooch through questionable means. As soon as you get it you disappear.

Hook — you have a mooch on line and are reeling him and his money in.

Independent Location Agreement — form that location signs to accept placement of vending machine or display.

L.R.A. — Location Request Agreement. A form that is sent to the mooch. He signs it requesting locating work.

Location list — form that the mooch signs. It lists all the locations that his displays are in.

Locator — person who finds locations for vending machines and displays.

Loose — refers to a nonbinding location placement form.

Money reach — first phase of the biz-op scam.

Mooch — person being screwed.

Mooch bait — samples of product or marketing pamphlet that is sent to the mooch.

Mooch fleecing — taking the mooch's money.

Mooch hit list — a list of suckers you have screwed.

Mooch points — things that help you sell the mooch.

Mooch real estate — an easy area to place displays at.

Mooch report — singers tell biz-opper how mooch is responding to the bait.

N.A.F. — National Awareness Foundation. A charity that locators use.

N.F.B. — National Federation of the Blind. A charity that locators use.

Offing — getting rid of.

Paying point — you pay another biz-opper 10% of anything over $5000.

Placement Agreement — form that location signs accepting vending machine or display.

Re-buy vends — to buy back vending machines you have sold a mooch.

Relocate — to find a replacement location for an unprofitable location.

Sell before you buy — a method biz-oppers use to get the mooch's money before they have the product.

Singer — a person who lies to the mooch about the product the biz-opper is selling.

Singer set-up — getting the mooch primed and ready to talk to the biz-opper's singer.

Spinners — a display that sits on the floor and can be rotated. It holds the mooch's merchandise.

Starter kit — a kit sent to a bon-bon eater. The starter kit supposedly contains all the product she needs to start her own home assembly factory.

Tag — a flaw in the mooch's contract that allows the biz-opper to break the contract.

Tour — to take a mooch to his locations.

Underground money — illegal tax-free money.

Upright vend — large floor model vending machine.

Work-at-home programs — an assembly oriented program that is sold to the housewife. Supposedly she is to get rich assembling products at home.

Appendix:
Business Opportunity Contracts,
Charity Forms,
Locating Agreements, Etc.

◆ ◆ ◆ ◆ ◆ ◆ ◆ ◆ ◆

Forms are in numerical order.

14. Location Agreement Contract (for vending machines). Contract the mooch signs that guarantees his locations. (page 153)
15. Limited Warranty Agreement (for displays and equipment). Contract the mooch signs that guarantees his locations. (pages 154-155)
16. Assigned Location Company Agreement (generic for all equipment). Contract the mooch signs that guarantees his locations. (page 156)
17. Independent Location Agreement. Agreement that location signs when accepting displays. (page 157)
18. Placement Agreement. Agreement that location signs when accepting displays. (page 158)
19. Location Agreement. Agreement that location signs when accepting displays. (page 159)
20. Telephone Agreement. Agreement that location signs for pay phone. (page 160)
21. Verification of Pay Phone Revenue. Statement that shows how much money the pay phone is generating. Always pick these up. Even though the phones are very seldom installed, it helps to get the locating money out of the mooch. (page 161)
22. Location List. Form that you use to list all of the mooch's locations. (page 162)
23. Location Understanding. Form that basically states that the locator will not be back to relocate. This is a tag form. If you get the mooch to sign it, his 90-day warranty form isn't worth beans. (page 163)

VANAF490A

VENDOR'S AGREEMENT

This AGREEMENT made th:: _____ day of _____ , 19_____ , by and between the NATIONAL AWARENESS FOUNDATION (hereinafter referred to as "NAF"), Suite 900, 601 Pennsylvania Avenue, Washington, DC 20004, (202) 737-4847, and...

_____
(hereinafter referred to as "VENDOR")

Address: _____ ZIP_____

Telephone Numbers: _____

Number of Locations: _____   Type of Equipment: _____

Date of 1st Billing: _____   Service Message Size: _____

Vending Company Agent: _____   Representative: _____

WITNESSETH:

WHEREAS, NAF is a corporation incorporated in Delaware in 1986 as a non-profit and having obtained IRS 501(c)(3) tax exemption March 20, 1989 from the IRS
Brooklyn Office, New York. The tax exempt number is 52-1493409. The vision of the work of NAF and its trademarked HUGS NOT DRUGS project is to alter the
conversation for ending the demand for drugs for school-age children, 7 through 12, by early education. NAF provides a technology for families to create differ-
ence-making conversations, networks the technology to organizations who are committed to alcohol and other drug abuse prevention, and conducts forums for
public awareness. NAF participates in a variety of forums and international conferences. While the project is not targeted towards schools, NAF provides the technology to community action groups who work with youth and, in particular, provides the work direct to families.

WHEREAS, the VENDOR is engaged in his or her own business of operation and distribution of Vending Equipment,

NOW THEREFORE, in consideration of the mutual promises and covenants set forth herein, and each intending to be legally-bound hereby, NAF and VENDOR
agree as follows:

1. The VENDOR agrees to display the NAF service message on each piece of its Equipment. VENDOR will use its best efforts to obtain commercial locations
   and assistance in placement of Equipment bearing the service message. Nothing in this Agreement shall be construed to create a partnership or joint venture
   or similar enterprise between VENDOR and NAF.

2. NAF grants VENDOR the right to use the name and logo of NAF in the form provided by NAF, to place on the Equipment of the VENDOR. NAF will provide
   the VENDOR with a Letter of Authorization (LOA), service message stickers with the NAF logo and, make available a price list of sample materials, if requested,
   of other promotional material approved by the Foundation. For more information, write NAF Processing Center, Suite 210, 7 Great Valley Parkway, Malvern,
   Pennsylvania 19355 or NAF Processing Center, Southeastern, Pennsylvania 19399-0585.

3. VENDOR may represent to owners and operators of commercial space and/or government installations NAF has authorized the VENDOR to enroll owners
   and operators to participate in facilitating display of the service message, and the VENDOR will make monthly financial remittances to NAF in accordance
   with this Agreement.

4. VENDOR will only use authorized NAF promotional material or literature. VENDOR will hold NAF harmless against any claim or liability including expenses
   arising from the unauthorized use of NAF's name or literature, or any other unauthorized use or representational information, procedure or promotional event
   in the marketing effort.

5. Each 6 month period (180 days), VENDOR will provide NAF with a list of all locations of the equipment placed. NAF will provide at no expense replacement
   stickers, if lost or damaged or otherwise rendered impractical for use by writing to NAF Processing and making a request.

6. The VENDOR indemnifies and holds NAF harmless from any and all claims and liabilities should they arise out of activity by the VENDOR in furtherance of
   the Agreement, from any acts or omission of its agents or employees or from the operation or installation of its equipment. The VENDOR also indemnifies
   and holds NAF harmless against all claim or liability arising from the product or services it sells. VENDOR agrees to obtain any insurance necessary to fulfill
   any condition or term of this Agreement, if necessary.

7. VENDOR agrees to remit NAF a monthly fee of _____ for use of the stickers and VENDOR has the option of remitting greater than the agreed-upon fee.
   Unless otherwise agreed, a sum equal to $2.00 per location per unit is due beginning 60 days from the first of the month following delivery of the Equipment
   to the VENDOR for placement. NAF will provide return-addressed envelopes to the Processing Center upon approval of this Agreement.

8. VENDOR shall be responsible fully for obtaining appropriate locations for each placement of equipment bearing the HUGS NOT DRUGS service message.
   VENDOR shall also be responsible for the maintenance and on-going operation by servicing the client in a manner associated with good business practices.
   In the event NAF deems action is required for failure of the VENDOR to perform on a timely basis under the terms of this Agreement, NAF may elect to notify
   each individual location of its intention to withdraw its participation and the HUGS NOT DRUGS service message.

*1.   **Charity Contract for the National Awareness Foundation (N.A.F.). (Page 1)***

9. VENDOR acknowledges NAF is not a part of any Agreement between the Agent marketing the vending Equipment and the VENDOR, nor is the VENDOR purchasing Equipment predicated on any representations other than those known and agreed to by NAF in writing. VENDOR agrees to be responsible for compliance with any federal, state, or local regulatory, registration, or bonding, if necessary, including taxes, legal expenses, licensing, for any and all aspects of its operation where statutorily mandated.

10. This Agreement shall extend for a five (5) year term renewable, unless or in the event notice is given 90 days preceding the end of the term. VENDOR agrees not to affiliate within one year of termination with any similar organizations in the field of alcohol or other drug abuse prevention and educational projects. If at any time notice is given for termination, all materials provided by the Foundation shall be returned at once by the VENDOR to NAF.

11. Either party may terminate this Agreement for cause by giving notice of termination to the other. Termination shall be in writing by certified mail return receipt requested. The party breaching the Agreement shall have ninety days to rectify any breach and, in that event, this Agreement shall remain in full force and effect. In the event of termination for cause without rectification, VENDOR agrees to return the NAF Letter of Authorization (LOA), remove NAF service message stickers, and return any and all other NAF promotional material.

12. SPECIAL PROMOTIONAL PROJECTS: By creating public awareness through the display of the HUGS NOT DRUGS service message, inquiries are created for producing drug educational and prevention projects. NAF invites your participation or inquiries for producing projects for committed organizations conducting community educational and prevention work for families. Special compensation by the Foundation for fundraising projects are available on a case basis. Write NAF for more information.

13. In the event any paragraph or part thereof of this Agreement conflicts with the law under which this Agreement is to be construed or, if any paragraph or part thereof be held invalid by a court of jurisdiction, such paragraph or part thereof shall be deleted from this Agreement and the Agreement shall be construed to give full effect to the remaining paragraphs or parts thereof.

14. This Agreement constitutes the entire Agreement between the parties. No change or modification of the Agreement shall be valid unless the same be in writing and signed by all the parties hereto. This Agreement shall not be amended, altered, or qualified, except by a memorandum in writing signed by both parties. NAF and VENDOR agree interpretation, enforcement and construction of this Agreement shall be governed by the laws of the State of Pennsylvania and all disputes which may arise under this Agreement shall be settled in a forum in the State of Pennsylvania.

15. This Agreement shall inure to the benefit of and be binding upon the parties and their respective heirs, personal representatives, administrators, successors, and assigns. The parties signing this Agreement on behalf of their respective entities have the authority to produce binding Agreements.

NATIONAL AWARENESS FOUNDATION:

_____   _____

Director & Senior Staff Writer   Director of Project Development

VENDOR:

Signed: _____   Date: _____

Print Name: _____

Signed: _____   Date: _____

Print Name: _____

Signed: _____   Date: _____

Print Name: _____

1.   Charity Contract for the National Awareness Foundation (N.A.F.). (Page 2)

"early education makes the difference"

Ruth S. Harris
Director

LOCATING AGREEMENT FOR VENDING OUTREACH

Thank you for agreeing to participate in the Vending Program of the **HUGS NOT DRUGS** project of the National Awareness Foundation, by allowing the placement of a vending machine on your premises which bears our service message. The monthly service fees we receive from the operators of these machines (regardless of any product sales) is making a significant improvement in the programs we are able to provide. Those who read our service message which appears on each machine put us in contact with many who may need our services for drug education and prevention projects. Should you decide at any time you no longer desire to participate in our Vending Program, simply call the person who placed the machine and it will be cheerfully removed.

Your signature below simply indicates your willingness to participate in our Vending Outreach Program and implies no liability or continuing obligation on your part.

BUSINESS NAME: _____

ADDRESS: _____ **ZIP:** _____

TELEPHONE NUMBERS: (___) _____ (___) _____

APPROVED BY: _____ **(Signed)**

NAME OF LOCATOR (PRINT): _____ **DATE:** _____

OPERATOR APPROVAL: _____

TELEPHONE (LOCAL): _____

THANK YOU!!

NAF Communications: 601 Pennsylvania Ave., Washington, DC 20004

2. *National Awareness Foundation Locating Agreement.*

NATIONAL FEDERATION OF THE BLIND

CONTRACT

This contract is made this_____ day of_____, 19 ____ by and between the National Federation of the Blind, 1800 Johnson Street, Baltimore, Maryland 21230, (a body corporate incorporated under the laws of the District of Columbia, hereinafter referred

to as "NFB") and _____
          Company Name   Owners Name

_____
          Address   City   State   Zip

_____ (hereinafter referred to as the "VENDOR").
          Home Phone   Work Phone

WHEREAS, the VENDOR is engaged in the operation and distribution of coin operated vending machines, and

WHEREAS, the NFB is engaged in the direction and coordination of research into the nature of blindness and the proper methods for eliminating the disadvantages arising from blindness, and the NFB undertakes programs to locate blind persons in need of information and assistance, and works to promote independence and stimulate the capabilities of blind people.

NOW THEREFORE, in consideration of the mutual promises and covenants set forth herein, the receipt and sufficiency of which are hereby acknowledged, the parties agree and promise as follows:

1. The VENDOR agrees to participate in the Vending Outreach Program of the NFB by displaying the outreach and service message of the NFB on its vending machines. The VENDOR will use its best efforts to obtain from stores, shopping centers, and other commercial locations and government installations, assistance in the placement of vending machines bearing the outreach and service message of the NFB.

2. The NFB hereby grants permission to the VENDOR to use the name and logo of the NFB on vending machines placed by the VENDOR. The NFB will provide the VENDOR with identifying material suitable for placement on vending machines containing the name and service message of the NFB. The VENDOR agrees to place this identifying material on vending machines in a manner approved by the NFB. This identifying material will give the name and address of the NFB and will inform readers that for emergencies or assistance involving blindness they may contact the NFB.

3. The parties agree that the VENDOR may represent to owners and operators of commercial space and government installations that:
   a. The NFB has authorized the VENDOR to participate in its Vending Outreach Program by displaying the service message of the NFB on its vending machines.
   b. The NFB has authorized the VENDOR to urge the owners and operators of commercial establishments and government installations to participate in the Vending Outreach Program of the NFB by permitting the VENDOR to place its vending machines bearing the outreach and service message of the NFB on his or her premises.
   c. The VENDOR will (regardless of proceeds from the machines) make fixed agreed upon monthly financial contributions to the NFB in return for the opportunity to participate in this outreach program.

4. The NFB will provide the VENDOR with literature stating that the VENDOR has been authorized to participate in its Vending Outreach Program as outlined herein. The VENDOR will not use the name of the NFB or literature of the NFB in any way which has not been specifically authorized by the NFB. The VENDOR will hold the NFB harmless against any claim or liability arising from the unauthorized use of its name or literature. The VENDOR will provide a list of the locations of vending machines to the NFB. This list will be updated on a quarterly basis.

5. The NFB shall not, without the prior written consent of the VENDOR, authorize or permit any other persons to place machines vending a similar product or service within those stores, or other commercial enterprises or government installations in which the VENDOR has already placed machines bearing the service message of the NFB.

6. The VENDOR hereby indemnifies and holds the NFB harmless from any and all claims and liability which may arise out of any activities of the VENDOR in furtherance of this contract, from any acts or omissions of its agents or employees, or from the operation of its vending machines. The VENDOR also indemnifies the NFB against any claim or liability arising from the products or services it sells. The VENDOR will provide the NFB with such financial surety as is satisfactory to the NFB.

7. The VENDOR hereby covenants to pay to the NFB a contribution of

8. The VENDOR shall be responsible for obtaining suitable locations for the placement of vending machines bearing the service message of the NFB. The VENDOR shall also be responsible for the placement, maintenance, and operation of vending machines, and shall in all cases give those with whom machines have been placed a method whereby he or she can be reached between regular service calls to deal with any problems which may arise. The machines shall contain fresh product and be in good working order.

9. During the five (5) year term of this contract and all subsequent five year terms, the VENDOR agrees that it will not work with any other organization of or for the blind and that it will, in the field of blindness, have an exclusive relationship with the NFB.

3.   *Charity Contract for the National Federation of the Blind (N.F.B.). (Page 1)*

10. This agreement shall be for a term of five (5) years. Either party may terminate this agreement, for cause, by giving notice of termination to the other. Any termination shall be effective ninety (90) days after the date it was mailed. The party breaching this contract shall have sixty (60) days to rectify any breach from the date that notice of termination is mailed. If the breaching party rectifies the breach, this contract shall remain in full force and effect, and the notice of termination shall be void. If this agreement is terminated for cause, then the VENDOR agrees to return the letter of authorization for participation in the program and to remove and return all stickers bearing the service message of the NFB. VENDOR further agrees promptly to remove his or her machines from all commercial establishments and government installations in which they have been placed as a part of this program and to make no attempt to place machines in those locations for a period of one year from the date of removal.

11. This contract shall be automatically renewed unless one party gives notice to the other in writing, of its intention to terminate the agreement ninety (90) days prior to the expiration of the term.

12. Any notice permitted or required to be given hereunder to any party shall be in writing and shall be delivered personally or sent by certified mail, return receipt requested. Unless a party notifies the other that its address has changed, all notices shall be sent to the parties at their addresses listed above. All checks should be made payable to the National Federation of the Blind. **All routine correspondence and checks should be sent to 1743 E. Evergreen Street, Mesa, AZ 85203.**

13. This agreement constitutes the entire contract between the parties. Its making has not been induced by, and the parties do not rely upon any oral representations or writing not incorporated herein and made a part hereof. This contract shall not be amended, altered, or qualified except by a memorandum in writing signed by both parties.

14. This agreement shall inure to the benefit of and be binding upon the parties and their respective heirs, personal representatives, administrators, successors, and assigns. The parties signing this contract on behalf of their respective entities have made full and truthful representation that they have the authority to make binding contracts on behalf of their respective entities.

15. The parties agree that the interpretation, enforcement, and construction of this agreement shall be governed by the laws of the State of Maryland and that all disputes which arise under this agreement shall be settled in a forum in the State of Maryland.

IN WITNESS WHEREOF, the parties hereto have set their hands the day and year first above written.

NATIONAL FEDERATION OF THE BLIND
BY:

_____
NORMAN D. GARDNER, Ph.D., Program Manager, Vending Outreach Program

_____

VENDOR
BY:

_____
PRINT NAME

_____
SIGNATURE

_____
TITLE

_____
WITNESS

Number of machines purchased _____

Machines purchased from _____
                                                    Company

Machine manufacturer or type _____

PLEASE SEND THIS COMPLETED CONTRACT TO:
National Federation of the Blind
1743 E. Evergreen St., Mesa, AZ 85203
Please KEEP a copy for your records.

---

3. *Charity Contract for the National Federation of the Blind (N.F.B.). (Page 2)*

VENDING OUTREACH PROGRAM

National Federation of the Blind

LOCATION ACQUISITION AGREEMENT

Thank you for agreeing to participate in the Vending Outreach Program of the National Federation of the Blind by allowing the placement of a vending machine on your premises which bears our service message. The monthly contribution we receive from the operators of these machines (regardless of any product sales) is making a significant improvement in the programs we are able to provide to blind people. Those who have read our service message which appears on each machine have put us in contact with many blind people who need our services.

Should you decide at any time that you no longer desire to participate in our Vending Outreach Program, simply call the person who placed the machine and it will be cheerfully removed.

Your signature below simply indicates your willingness to participate in our Vending Outreach Program and implies no liability or continuing obligation on your part.

Business: _____

Address: _____

Phone: _____

Authorized Signature: _____

Please Print Name Clearly

Locator: _____

Date: _____

4.   National Federation of the Blind Locating Agreement.

AMERICAN ASSOCIATION FOR LOST CHILDREN, INC.

P.O. Box 41154
Houston, TX 77241
713-466-1852
FAX 713-937-6196
1-800-375-5683

American Association For Lost Children, Inc., the charity that finds and returns missing children, re-uniting them with their loved ones, operating exclusively on donations, and an adjunct service for all law enforcement agencies.

BOARD OF DIRECTORS

Mark Miller
Founder/President

Mike Kramer
Vice President/Director

Pam Kaiser
Enron Oil & Gas Corp.

Bobby Bates
Gannett Outdoor/Texas

Fernando Ruata
Pastor

Donna Rucker
Mother of found children in Tennessee

Jackie Gatewood
Mother of found children in Texas

Pam Dixon
ATC Longdistance

ADVISORY BOARD

Don Goates
Special Agent
U.S. Naval Investigations
Chorpus Christi, Texas

Richard & Linda Feller
Fundraising Coordinators

Guy Tutwiler
Former Chief of Police
Lavaca, Arkansas

Maria Nicholas
Mother of found child in Germany

Shirley Shirley
Grandmother of found child in Texas

CONTRACT

PLEASE PRINT

Vendor Name:_____

Address:_____

City & State:_____
Zip Code

Phone: Day(   )_____Eve._____

# of Displays_____

It is Agreed:

1. In return for Vending displays advertising AMERICAN ASSOCIATION FOR LOST CHILDREN, INC. (AALC) the vendor agrees to make fixed monthly payments to AALC (regardless of proceeds from the displays).

2. The vendor agrees to pay AALC a contribution of one fifty (1.50) per display on location per month. (ex:12 displays = 18.00 month)

3. Upon AALC's receipt of signed contract and 1st monthly payment, labels for displays will be issued. Regular payments will then begin 60 days after date of contract. **MAKE CHECKS PAYABLE TO AALC***

4. Contract is valid from date on contract for as long as vendor advertises AALC. AALC needs a written notice of sale of vending displays or termination of contract.

5. The vendor hereby indemnifies and holds AALC harmless from any and all claims and liabilities.

6. If the vendor breaches this contract the vendor will have 60 days to rectify the breach. Please keep in touch, AALC wants to work with you. If not rectified further action will be taken.

7. Vendor Signature:_____

   AALC Signature:_____

   Date_____

PLEASE SPECIFY ON CHECK - 'VENDING CHECK'
*WHERE DID YOU HEAR ABOUT A.A.L.C.?_____

Do not love the world, nor the things in the world. If anyone loves the world, the love of the Father is not in him. 1 John 2:15

5.   *Charity Contract for the American Association of Lost Children, Inc.*

 American Association For Lost Children, Inc.

The Charity That Finds & Returns Missing Children

Mark Miller
Founder/President

LOCATING AGREEMENT FOR VENDING OUTREACH

Thank you for agreeing to participate in the Vending Program of the **American Association For Lost Children, Inc.**, by allowing the placement of a vending machine on your premises which bears our service message. The monthly service fees we receive from the operators of these machines (regardless of any product sales) is making a significant improvement in the programs we are able to provide. Those who read our service message which appears on each machine put us in contact with many who may need our services. Should you decide at any time you no longer desire to participate in our Vending Program, simply call the person who placed the machine and it will be cheerfully removed.

Your signature below simply indicates your willingness to participate in our Vending Outreach Program and implies no liability or continuing obligation on your part.

BUSINESS NAME: _____

ADDRESS: _____ ZIP: _____

TELEPHONE NUMBERS: (___) _____ (___) _____

APPROVED BY: _____ (Signed)

NAME OF LOCATOR (PRINT): _____ DATE: _____

OPERATOR APPROVAL: _____

TELEPHONE (LOCAL): _____

THANK YOU!!

American Association for Lost Children, Inc. • PO Box 41154 • Houston, Texas 77241 • 1-800-375-5683

6. *American Association of Lost Children, Inc. Locating Agreement.*

**Search
Reports**

Central Registry For The Missing.

AGREEMENT

This agreement made this _____ day of _____, 1990, by and between Search Reports, Inc., (a body corporate incorporated under the laws of the State of New Jersey, hereinafter referred to as "Search"), and _____

(business name) _____

(address) _____

(city, state & zip code) _____

(area code & phone no.) _____ (hereinafter referred to as the "Vendor").

WHEREAS, the Vendor is engaged in the operation and distribution of coin operated vending machines, and

WHEREAS, Search is engaged in the endeavor of helping to locate missing individuals and has received an Internal Revenue Service tax exemption under Section 501 (c)(3) of the Internal Revenue Code.

NOW, THEREFORE, in consideration of the mutual promises and covenants set forth herein, the receipt and sufficiency of which are hereby acknowledged, the parties agree and promise as follows:

1. The Vendor will use its best efforts to obtain from stores, shopping centers, and other commercial locations, donation of space and place machines purchased from Universal Vending Corporation on location with the Search logo.

2. Search hereby grants permission to the Vendor to use the name and logo of Search on vending machines placed by the Vendor. Search will provide the Vendor with identifying material suitable for placement on vending machines containing the name of Search. The Vendor agrees to place this identifying material on vending machines in a manner approved by Search. This identifying material will give the name and address of Search, will state that space has been donated to Search for the placement of the vending machines, and will inform readers that for assistance involving Search they may call or write Search.

   a. Identifying material in the form of self-adhesive Search logo and message stickers provided for Vendor use are and shall remain the property of Search.

3. The parties agree that the Vendor may represent to owners and operators of commercial space that:

   a. Search has authorized the Vendor to solicit donations to Search of commercial space for the placement of vending machines; and

   b. The Vendor will pay Search a fixed, agreed upon monthly contribution towards the work of finding the missing.

4. Search will provide the Vendor with literature stating that the Vendor has been authorized to solicit the donation of commercial space for placement of vending machines by Search. The Vendor will not use the name of Search or literature of Search in any way which has not been specifically authorized by Search. The Vendor will hold Search harmless against any claim or liability arising from the unauthorized use of its name or literature. The Vendor will provide a list of the locations of vending machines to Search. This list will be updated on a quarterly basis.

5. Search shall not, without the prior consent of the Vendor, authorize or permit any other persons to solicit for its benefit, space for the placement of similar machines vending comparable products within those locations in which the Vendor has already placed machines bearing the name of Search provide that Search shall have been previously notified of the placement of the machines.

6. The Vendor hereby indemnifies and holds Search harmless from any and all claims and liability which may arise out of any activities of the Vendor in futherance of this Agreement, from any acts or omissions of its agents or employees, or from the operation of its vending machines. The Vendor also indemnifies Search against any claim or liability arising from the products or services it sells.

7. The Vendor hereby covenants to pay to Search a fee of Two Dollars and Fifty Cents ($2.50) per machine per month with payment to be made monthly in advance.

8. The Vendor agrees that the number and type of machines shown below shall be the basis for this agreement initially and that the Vendor may extend the number of machines using the name and logo of Search, if so desired, under the same terms as 7., above.

9. By virtue of this Agreement, Search hereby assigns to the Vendor all space donated to it for the placement of vending machines for the purposes contemplated by this Agreement.

10. The Vendor shall be responsible for obtaining donations of space to Search. The Vendor shall also be responsible for the placement, maintenance, and operation of vending machines.

11. This agreement shall be for a term of five (5) years. Either party may terminate this Agreement, for cause, by giving notice of termination to the other. Any termination shall be effective ninety (90) days after the date it was mailed. The party breaching this Agreement shall have sixty (60) days to rectify any breach from the date that notice of termination is mailed. If the breaching party rectifies the breach, this Agreement shall remain in full force and effect, and the notice of termination shall be void.

7. Contract for Search Reports. (Page 1)

12. This Agreement shall be automatically renewed unless one party gives notice to the other in writing, of its intention to terminate the Agreement ninety (90) days prior to the expiration of the term.

13. If any term of this Agreement is or becomes void, voidable, or unenforceable for any reason whatsoever, then that provision or those provisions shall be deemed severed from the rest of the Agreement and all provisions thereof shall remain in full force and effect.

14. Any notice permitted or required to be given hereunder to any party shall be in writing and shall be delivered personally or sent by certified mail, return receipt requested. Unless a party notifies the other that its address has changed, all notices shall be sent to the addresses of the parties as set forth in this Agreement.

15. This Agreement constitutes the entire Agreement between the parties. Its making has not been induced by, and the parties do not rely upon any oral representations or writing not Incorporated herein and made a part hereof. This Agreement shall not be amended, altered, or qualified except by a memorandum in writing signed by both parties.

16. This Agreement shall insure to the benefit of and be binding upon the parties and their respective heirs, personal representatives, administrators, successors, and assigns.

17. This Agreement has been made at Hasbrouck Heights, New Jersey. The parties agree that the laws of the State of New Jersey shall apply to its interpretation and enforcement.

IN WITNESS WHEREOF, the parties hereto have set their hands the day and year first above written.

ATTEST: _____

_____

Type of Machines Purchased _____

Number Machines Purchased _____

SEARCH REPORTS, INC.

By: _____

VENDOR:

By: _____

_____

_____

_____

Search Reports, Inc. • 345 Boulevard • Hasbrouck Heights • New Jersey 07604 • Tel: (201) 288-4445

7.   Contract for Search Reports. (Page 2)

LOCATION CONSIGNMENT AGREEMENT
(Print All Information)

DATE: _____

NAME OF LOCATION: _____

LOCATION ADDRESS: _____

CITY: _____ STATE: _____ ZIP: _____

PHONE: (_____) _____

OWNER/MANAGER: _____

The LOCATION OWNER/MANAGER agrees as follows:

1) To furnish space for a self-standing Outreach Toy Display Rack complete with an assortment of toys and/ or stuffed toys; that this merchandise is on consignment memo with said location indicated above until sold. Signed copies will be maintained by both parties.

2) That the Outreach Toy Display Distributor is the owner of said merchandise and that the undersigned location Owner/Manager agrees to use his or her best efforts to sell this merchandise for cash at the price indicated on each item.

3) To pay the Outreach Distributor for all items sold or missing at the time of inventory verification and restocking.

4) To receive full payment a commission equal to _____% of the gross sales (exclusive of sales tax) of items sold from this display rack.

5) That the Outreach Distributor will maintain the Toy Display Rack and regularly visit the location indicated above in order to promptly restock the display rack.

6) To have the right to request removal of Outreach Toy Display Rack(s) and merchandise at any time, with reasonable prior notice, and will not permit the removal of said toy display rack and merchandise by anyone other than the Outreach Distributor of his agent.

7) That all outstanding consignment memos be paid in full as specified in item 3 above.

Accepted and Approved By: _____
(Authorized Location Owner/Manager Signature)

OUTREACH DISTRIBUTOR NAME:_____ DATE: _____

ADDRESS:_____ PHONE: (__ _____)_____

CITY: _____ STATE: _____ ZIP: _____

OUTREACH DISTRIBUTOR: _____ _____
(Signature)

No. of Toy Display Racks At This Location: _____

Type of Unit: **TOY DISPLAY RACK**

Name of Charitable Organization: **SEARCH REPORTS, INC.**

Store Hours: Weekdays: _____ AM to _____ PM

SAT: _____ AM to _____ PM   SUN: _____ AM to _____ PM

8.   *Consignment Agreement for Search Reports Toy Displays.*

DISTRIBUTOR PURCHASE AGREEMENT

DATE _____

Purchaser_____
                              NAME   PHONE NO.

Correspondence
Address: _____
                  STREET   CITY   STATE   ZIP CODE

Shipping
Address: _____
                  STREET NO.   CITY   STATE   ZIP CODE

1.   **TERMS AND CONDITIONS**
      The buyer or Purchaser herein shall be denoted as the "Distributor" and
              shall herein be denoted as the "Company".

2. , **DELIVERIES:** Displays and supplies described in this agreement shall be delivered promptly by the Company,
      providing that full payment has been received by the Company. Shipment shall be made within 30 days from the
      date the displays and supplies are ordered, except in cases of freight line and/or labor strikes, material shortages,
      order backlogs or other contingencies over which the Company exercises no control.

3   **FEE:** Distributor hereby agrees to pay Company herewith, in certified funds, the sum of _____
      _____($_____ DOLLARS.)
      representing the entire amount due by Distributor to the Company for the initial inventory shipment of Products.

      _____

      _____

      _____

      Distributor agrees to pay an initial deposit of $_____
      and the balance due of $_____ upon acceptance of the Company, **IN CERTIFIED FUNDS.**

4   **FREIGHT:** Shipments shall be made F.O.B. our warehouse or factory and freight costs are to be paid by the
      Distributor, who agrees to accept goods immediately upon arrival.

5   **PRODUCT:** The Company shall produce a continuous supply of product which shall be made available for
      purchase by Distributor at wholesale prices which shall be published and delivered to Distributor from time to time.

6   **DISTRIBUTORSHIP:** The Company appoints Distributor, on a non-exclusive basis, with Marketing Responsibility
      in the following area:

      _____

      Distributor understands that Company has no involvement whatsoever in securing retail locations.

7   **LIMITATIONS:** The Distributor is an independent contractor and not an employee or agent of the Company and
      shall not use the Company's name for the procurement of credit and shall in no way conduct his business in a
      manner which may prove detrimental to the good name of the Company.

H   **COMPLETE CONTRACT:** This purchase agreement is complete within itself. The Distributor is not relying on
      written expressions, promises or warranties made by anyone regarding this transaction, except those expressly
      stated herein. The Distributor acknowledges that no one has the authority to alter the written terms of this
      agreement.

9.   **ACCEPTANCE:** This Distributor Agreement is subject to acceptance by an officer of the Company at its offices in
              and if so accepted it shall be deemed executed, binding, non-cancelable and business
      transacted in   Should the Distributor applicant not be accepted by the Company as Distributor,
      the Company shall return, via Registered Mail, all monies on deposit within (5) business days from the date.

10.   Distributor acknowledges that he/she has complete control of his/her method of sales and/or marketing. Any
      suggested procedures and/or sales/marketing plans and strategies furnished to Distributor by the Company are
      furnished solely for convenience and information purposes and are not mandatory. The Distributor shall have
      complete control over sources of supply and services: however, Distributor will not market or display products or
      equipment of any kind from any other source other than Company while using Company's name, trademark, logos,
      samples, trade name or equipment.

9.   Distributor Purchase Agreement. (Page 1)

11. Company agrees to respect the confidentiality and privacy of Distributor and further agrees that it will not use the name and/or address of Distributor for any sale or as an implied endorsement.

12. **NO WAIVER:** Failure by either party hereto to enforce at any time any term under this Agreement shall not be a waiver of that party's right to thereafter enforce each and every term and condition of this Agreement.

13. **SUCCESSORS AND ASSIGNS:** The rights and remedies of Company under this Agreement shall inure to the successors and assigns of Company. Distributor shall have no right to assign, transfer or otherwise dispose of its right, title and interest in and to any part of this Agreement or to assign or delegate the burdens hereof, without the prior written consent of Company, which consent shall not be unreasonably withheld. Distributor's obligations here under shall survive any termination or expiration of this Agreement.

14. **ATTORNEY'S FEES:** In the event of any litigation concerning any dispute between the parties arising out of or relating to this Agreement, Company shall be entitled to recover from Distributor all expenses, attorney's fees and costs incurred therein or in the enforcement or collection of any judgement rendered therein, unless the Court determined Distributor to have prevailed in all matters. Further, the Distributor shall pay all expenses and all attorney's fees incurred by the Company and/or Company's Affiliates in connection with any default hereunder, whether or not litigation is commenced by reason thereof.

15. **SEVERABILITY:** If any provision or provisions of the Agreement shall be held to be wholly or partially invalid, illegal or unenforceable, the validity, legality and enforceability of the remaining provisions shall in no way be affected or impaired thereby; it being the intent of all parties that to the extent provisions otherwise enforceable, invalid or illegal may be construed or limited by a Court or tribunal so as to allow for partial enforceability, said provisions shall be so enforced.

16. **GOVERNING LAWS AND JURISDICTION:** This Agreement shall be governed as to all matters, including validity, construction and performance by the laws of the State of   and Distributor hereby submits to the jurisdiction of the Courts in and for said State (with venue to be in   should Company elect, with respect to any particular dispute under or related to this Agreement to have same adjudicated in Illinois.

17. **NOTICE:** Any notice under this Agreement shall be given prepaid, certified mail, or prepaid telegram or personally delivered at the addressees set forth above or such addresses as either party shall hereinafter furnish to the other in writing. If the communication is mailed, delivery shall be deemed complete the earlier of (a) three (3) days after the communications is placed in the United States mail or (b) on the date actually received.

18. **FRANCHISE LAWS:** Each party agrees that this Agreement is not intended to, and does not, constitute the sale of a franchise prohibited by any state or federal laws. Each party understands the rights provided by such laws and each party specifically waives any and all rights otherwise available to it under those laws.

19. **PARAGRAPH HEADINGS:** The headings of the several paragraphs of this Agreement are inserted solely for the convenience of reference and are not a part of, and are not intended to govern, limit or aid in the construction of any term or provision hereof.

SPECIAL INSTRUCTIONS: _____

_____

_____

_____

_____

I HAVE READ THIS DISTRIBUTOR AGREEMENT THOROUGHLY AND UNDERSTAND ALL ITS TERMS AND CONDITIONS AND HEREBY ACKNOWLEDGE RECEIPT OF COPY OF SAME.

SIGNATURE OF DISTRIBUTOR_____ PHONE(   )_____

INDEPENDENT REPRESENTATIVE_____

APPROVED AND ACCEPTED IN   THIS_____ DAY OF _____ 19_____

_____ TITLE _____

9. *Distributor Purchase Agreement. (Page 2)*

CONTRACT

1. PARTIES TO THIS PURCHASE AGREEMENT HEREINAFTER REFERRED TO AS "AGREEMENT".

The parties to the agreement are _____ herein referred to as Company, and
_____hereinafter referred to as
"Purchaser".

2. TERMS AND CONDITIONS:

Company hereby sells and Purchaser hereby purchases the following described merchandise, subject to the terms and conditions as set forth herein. Purchaser agrees to pay all sales use taxes, if applicable, as a result of the purchase of said merchandise from company.

QUANTITY	DESCRIPTION	PRICE	TOTAL

Company guarantees not to sell to any purchaser other than Purchaser herein named in the territory as follows:_____
_____
_____

for a period of (   ) days. Purchaser has FIRST RIGHT of refusal for expansion in said territory.

3. DELIVERY:

Merchandise described in this Agreement shall be shipped within 30 working days of acceptance of this agreement by the Company and payment in full. Company shall not be liable for delays that may be caused by acts of God, strikes, fire, material shortage, or for any reason beyond the control of the Company. Delivery in all cases will be effected without delay by Company.

4. FREIGHT CHARGES:

All prices are F.O. B. point of departure.

5. ETHICS:

It is understood that this is not a franchise offering nor a security offering, and the Purchaser shall operate as an independent contractor. This Agreement will be governed by the laws of the State of

6. It is understood and agreed that no agency is created by reason of this Agreement or otherwise between Company and Purchaser, that Purchaser shall not in any respect act for Company, and that Purchaser shall at all times act as an Independent Contractor only. Further, Purchaser agrees to use his own name, his own trade name, or to call his company by any name he desires so long as it in no way relates to COMPANY'S name or to COMPANY. Purchaser is responsible for any license fees, bonds or taxes if applicable.

7. WARRANTY:

One year warranty for defective workmanship.

8. Purchaser agrees to pay Company concurrently with execution of this Agreement a deposit of_____for_____, machine(s). Balance of_____ _____ to be paid concurrently with execution of this Agreement made payable to _____
Escrow Account. All checks must be in the form of a certified or Cashier's Check. Monies made payable to   Escrow account to be held is escrow at the Bank of   for release **after** shipment.

9. Company and Purchaser agree that this Purchase Order contains the entire understanding of the Agreement between the parties and there is no reliance upon any verbal representation what soever. Company is not guaranteeing or representing any minimum or maximum earnings. Earnings are primarily dependent upon the service and sales volume of locations and factors beyond the control of the Company. Company does not furnish locations for merchandise described in this agreement.

ENFORCEMENT:

This agreement is entered into in the State of   and shall be construed and enforced in accordance with the laws of such state.

Executed this_____day of _____, 19_ _____.

_____
Purchasers Name (Please Print)

_____
Purchaser's Signature

_____
Address

_____
City /State/Zip/Phone

_____
Company's Agent

The foregoing Agreement accepted at
this _____,
day of_____, 19_____.

BY:_____

Title:_____

10. Purchaser Contract.

BUYER'S INVENTORY PURCHASE ORDER

Buyer's Name:_____

Address: _____

City:_____ State: _____ Zip Code:_____

Business Phone #: _____ Home Phone#:_____

SELLER:

Quantity	Description	Price	Total
	Total Purchase Order		

1. SHIPPING

The Seller agrees to ship the equipment within twenty (20) working days from receipt of the Purchase Order accompanied by full payment in the form of a cashier's check, certified check, money order or bank transfer. Delivery shall be subject to and contingent upon, strikes, labor difficulties, fire, delay or defaults of common carriers, failure or curtailment in Seller's usual sources of supply, governmental decrees or orders, or any other delays beyond the Seller's reasonable control, and the Seller shall not be liable for any loss or damage arising therefrom. Buyer may cancel the order by written notice delivered to the Seller prior to shipment if the order is not delivered within forty-five (45) working days of receipt of the Purchase Order and payment. Shipping costs are Purchaser's obligation.

2. WARRANTY

The Manufacturer guarantees to replace or at its option to repair any products or parts thereof which are found to be defective in material or workmanship within one year from date of shipment. The obligation with respect to such products or parts shall be limited to replacement or repair F.O.B. manufacturer, and in no event shall the Seller be liable for consequential or special damages, or for transportation, installation, adjustment, or other expenses which may arise in connection with such products or parts. This warranty is expressly made in lieu of any and all other warranties expressed or implied, including the warranties of merchantability and fitness.

11. Buyer's Inventory Purchase Order. (Page 1)

3. **ENTIRE AGREEMENT**
   This agreement is intended by the parties as a final expression of their agreement and as a complete and exclusive statement of its terms. Buyer understands and agrees that Seller offers no buy-backs, money back guarantees, or refunds. Buyer agrees that buyer is not relying upon any verbal or written representation whatsoever, except as expressly set forth in this agreement. Buyer acknowledges and agrees that Seller does not guarantee or represent that   when installed, will guarantee any minimum earnings as the earnings of   are rendered by the Buyer, all of which factors are beyond the control of the Seller. No usage of trade shall be relevant or admissible to supplement. Agreement can only be modified in writing, signed by the parties, or their duly authorized agents.

4. **TRADEMARKS**
   Buyer understands and agrees that the name   and the literature and trakemarks are the property of

5. **SPECIAL PROVISIONS**

In witness whereof this Agreement has been executed by the parties on the date set forth adjacent to the signature of each party.

I ACKNOWLEDGE THAT I HAVE RECEIVED AND HAVE READ A COPY OF THE PROSPECTUS.

DATE: _____   _____

                                                 BUYER:

DATE: _____   _____

                                                 SELLER:
                                                 Authorized Representative of

11. Buyer's Inventory Purchase Order. (Page 2)

WHOLESALE PURCHASE ORDER

DATE_____/_____19____

(PURCHASER) NAME: _____

ADDRESS: _____

CITY: _____ STATE:_____ ZIP:_____

HOME PHONE: (   ) _____ BUSINESS: (   )_____

QUAN.	DESCRIPTION	EACH	TOTAL
		$	
		$	

QUANTITY DISCOUNT	$	
TOTAL DUE	CORP.	$
30% AMOUNT REMITTED	WITH ORDER	$
70% BALANCE DUE	UPON SHIPMENT	$

PLEASE ENTER MY ORDER FOR:

ALL ORDERS INCLUDE:

-
-

ALL FUNDS TO BE CERTIFIED CASHIERS CHECK OR MONEY ORDER!

SHIPPING AND HANDLING CHARGES NOT INCLUDED. INSTALLATION OF INVENTORY IS PURCHASER'S RESPONSIBILITY. ORDERS ARE NOT SUBJECT TO CANCELLATION. PAYMENTS ARE NON-REFUNDABLE. I UNDERSTAND THAT THIS IS AN ORDER FOR PRODUCT AND THAT NO GUARANTEES OF MINIMUM SALES HAVE BEEN MADE, IN WRITING OR VERBALLY. THE EXCLUSIVE JURISDICTION AND VENUE FOR ALL DISPUTES OR ACTIONS ARISING OUT OF THIS TRANSACTION SHALL BE

ACCEPTED FOR (

BY: _____ PURCHASER X_____

DATE ACCEPTED _____ PURCHASER X_____

12. *Wholesale Purchase Order.*

LETTER OF ACKNOWLEDGEMENT

INITIAL

The undersigned purchaser acknowledges the following:

———————— 1. I have received a copy of the purchase agreement which I have executed this day.

———————— 2. I have been given an opportunity to read the agreement that I have signed, and all other materials presented to me. If I have not fully read any of these materials, I have done so at my own risk, and not in reliance on any oral explanations offered by sales people with whom I have dealt.

———————— 3. I understand that the rights and responsibilities of the parties to this agreement shall be determined by the written document; I am not relying on oral representations, conversations, or statements made by any salesperson during the course of this transaction.

———————— 4. No promises of income or revenue has been made to me. I understand that the risk of profit or loss on this venture is mine and solely. I do not hold the company or its salespeople and officers responsible for achieving any level of income or profit.

———————— 5. No promises regarding locations or territories have been made to me, other than that which is set forth in the written agreement.

———————— 6. I, the undersigned, assume full responsibility for any and all, city, county, state, federal, taxes, license fees and regulations.

——————————————————   ——————————————————
purchaser   witnessed by

——————————————.   ——————————————
Dated   Dated

13. Letter of Acknowledgment.

LOCATION AGREEMENT

This Location Agreement is made this _____ day of _____, 199___, between   and

Name_____ Address _____

City _____ State _____ Zip _____

hereinafter referred to as Vendor.

In consideration of the non-refundable fee, as set forth herein, paid by Vendor to   the parties agree as follows:

1. _____ will provide Vendor with a location upon which to place Vendor's equipment. The location shall be subject to Vendor's approva⌐. This shall be the primary location.

2. If, after the expiration of sixty (60) days from the date Vendor's machine is placed and operating at the primary location, Vendor is dissatisfied with the primary location, _____ shall provide Vendor with an alternate location provided that ˋVendor has supplied _____ with the following documentation:

    (i) Weekly Vending Reports, at the expiration of each week commencing one (1) week after actual placement and operation of Vendor's machine. EQUIPMENT MUST BE INSTALLED WITHIN SEVEN (7) DAYS AFTER LOCATION IS SECURED;

    (ii) Records showing weekly servicing of each machine, commencing from the date of operation at the primary location;

    (iii) Written notification by Vendor expressing dissatisfaction with the primary location. This notification shall be sent via Certified Mail, Return/Receipt Requested and shall be postmarked no later than five (5) days after the sixty (60) day period.

    THERE SHALL BE NO RELOCATION IF ANY OF THE ABOVE CONDITIONS ARE NOT FULLY COMPLIED WITH.

3. _____ shall provide Vendor with an alternate location if the manager, owner or agent of the primary location refuses to allow the installation of the vending machine. INSTALLATION MUST BE ATTEMPTED WITHIN SEVEN (7) DAYS OF SECURING THE PRIMARY LOCATION.

    Number of Locations _____

    Types of Machines _____

    Location Fee Sent $ _____

    Amount Due $ _____

ALL FEES PAID PURSUANT TO THIS AGREEMENT ARE NON-REFUNDABLE.

The undersigned represent that they have read, understand and agree to the terms of this Agreement and further that they have full authority to enter into this Agreement.

SIGNED: _____

OWNER/OPERATOR

SIGNED: _____
BY: _____

14. *Location Agreement Contract (for vending machines).*

LIMITED WARRANTY

OR ANY LOCATOR WILL REPLACE ORIGINAL LOCATION UNDER A CONTRACT WITH _____ AT NO COSTS TO OWNER UNDER THE FOLLOWING TERMS AND CONDITIONS.

1.   This Limited Warranty covers only original service provided by _____ and documented by (a) Confirmation & Acceptance agreement, (b) Placement Verification & Acknowledgement agreement, (c) Placement Agreements. All documents must be accepted and approved by Owner and a part of their business records.

2.   This Limited Warranty DOES NOT cover any representations, warranties, sales claims or other assurances made to Owner by any person or company from whom Owner has purchased equipment nor any verbal promises made by anyone except those commitments in writing and made a part of this Limited Warranty and the agreements mentioned in Paragraph 1 of this document.

3.   The owner of equipment, displays or vendors is responsible for delivery, set up and service.

4.   Owner must install equipment in a timely manner of fifteen days (15) from date of acceptance of location Placement Agreements.

5.   This Limited Warranty is for a period of ninety (90) days from date posted on Placement Verification & Acknowledgement agreement.

6.   After compliance to Paragraph 4, service must be continuous and acceptable to the terms of the Placement Agreement until the termination date (90 days from date of acceptance of Placement Verification & Acknowledgement agreement) with proof of service provided in the following manner:
      (a)   Proof of service must be documented by a dated service receipt signed by the locations authorized person.
      (b)   Copies of "Proof of Service" receipts from each original location showing service being provided every week from date of installation until termination date of this Limited Warranty and mailed in a timely manner to $uccess $ystems within five days from date of service.

15. Limited Warranty Agreement (for displays and equipment). (Page 1)

      (c)   has the option to request and receive other supportive documents to verify Proof of Service if it considers receipts questionable.

7.   In the event a business changes or cancels a Placement Agreement within the grace period of fifteen days from the receipt of Placement Agreements and subject to Paragraph 4 that location shall be replaced under the same terms and conditions of this Limited Warranty.

8.   At the option of the Placement-Locator, in agreement with owner, extra locations can be presented and documented as replacements for the events in Paragraph 7, if they occur.

9.   All claims under this Limited Warranty shall be made in writing to   within the ninety (90) day term and only then will replacement locations be completed thirty (30) days following the termination date of this agreement and is limited to a one time replacement for each Placement Agreement.

10.   Any terms or conditions of this Limited Warranty that are not complied with becomes null and void by default. Notice of default by either party will be mailed by certified letter to the defaulting party.

11.   Any additions or deletions to this document will automatically make it null and void. Any disputes arising from performance or lack of it, the Laws of the State of   shall prevail.

Notice: Document is certified and validated when Owner & Locator signs below.

ACCEPTED BY OWNER:

_____

                                LOCATOR

DATE:_____

15. Limited Warranty Agreement (for displays and equipment). (Page 2)

ASSIGNED LOCATION COMPANY   **PURCHASER**

Assignment Date_____

_____   _____
Name   Name

_____   _____
Address   Address

_____   _____
City   State   Zip   City   State   Zip

_____   _____
Phone   Phone

_____doing business as an independent   the
purpose of which is to secure locations for

for

All locations are guaranteed by Locator   to the extent that they have agreed
to provide at no additional cost, a vendor replacement location after 90 days of actual
operation of a vendor, in any location provided by them for any of the following reasons:

A. Revenue from the displays is not sufficient to make it a profitable location for Company.
   This shall be determined after 90 days of actual operation of a display in any location
   secured for   "A Profitable location" shall be defined as any location
   yielding a minimum of   ~-les per day per location. This guarantee is made providing the
   following records are made available to Locator

   1. Records showing no less than once per week of ser .icing each.
   2. Receipts from suppliers showing orders.
   3. Agreed commission paid to location.

B. On the day of installation of the displays at a location secured by Locator/
   Company, the manager, and/or owner or person signing the location agreement, refuses
   for any reason to allow the display to be installed.

No other agreement or guarantee has been given or expressed. Locations have been verified
by Purchaser.

This contract completed _____, on this _____ day of _____19____.

Number of Locations _____.   Signed:_____
                                                       Assigned Company Operator

Type of Display: Signed:_____
                                                       Locator/

_____

Special Conditions:_____

_____

_____

16. Assigned Location Company Agreement (generic for all equipment).

Independent Location
Agreement

AGREEMENT

LOCATION _____ DATE_____

ADDRESS_____PHONE _____

CITY_____STATE_____ZIP_____

MACHINE_____MODEL_____

It is mutually agreed that the Independent Dealer, owner of the above machine, will install its machine at no cost or obligation to the location.

These machines and contents thereof, are the exclusive property of the Independent Dealer.

It is also agreed that the machine(s) may be removed at any time at the request of either party and that the machine(s) will be removed by the Independent Dealer only.

The Independent Dealer is responsible for maintenance, repairs, and insurance for theft and vandalism.

Management of Location agress to provide space for machines.

```
SPECIAL INSTRUCTIONS :




```

BY_____
(Authorization Signature)

BY_____
Acceptance of location
By Owner of equipment

BY_____
Locator Company Representative

17.   *Independent Location Agreement.*

PLACEMENT AGREEMENT

Placement Name _____ Phone No. _____

Address _____ City _____ State _____ Zip _____

Description _____ Commission _____

IT IS MUTUALLY AGREED BETWEEN ALL PARTIES THAT:

(1) ALL EQUIPMENT OR DISPLAYS WILL BE INSTALLED ON AN INDEFINITE BASIS AT NO COST OR OBLIGATION TO THE LOCATION.

(2) ANY PLACEMENT CAN BE REMOVED AT THE REQUEST OF EITHER PARTY PROVIDING REMOVAL IS BY ASSIGNEE ONLY.

(3) ASSIGNEE SHALL PROVIDE ACCEPTABLE SERVICE TO THE LOCATION, INCLUDING CLEANING, FILLING, AND COLLECTIONS AS NEEDED.

(4) THE LOCATION IS PROVIDING SPACE AND POWER, IF REQUIRED, FOR THE ABOVE DESCRIBED EQUIPMENT OR DISPLAY TO THE ASSIGNOR WHO WILL ASSIGN THIS AGREEMENT TO THE NAMED ASSIGNEE BELOW WHO IS RESPONSIBLE FOR ALL COMMISSIONS DUE LOCATION AS A CONDITION OF THIS AGREEMENT.

Location Approval _____ Title _____

Assignor Agent _____ For   INTERVEND

ASSIGNED TO: _____ Phone No. _____

Form 101-7/90 5M

18.   Placement Agreement.

LOCATION AGREEMENT

Location:

Name _____

Address _____ Phone _____

City _____ State _____ Zip _____

The above location hereby agrees to provide space for the following equipment:

Amount	Model	Displays.
_____	_____	_____

It is understood that the display owner will maintain all service requirements of the display. The location agrees to use reasonable effort to protect the display from external damage.

Title to the display shall remain in the name of the distributor, and he/she or his/her agent may at any time take possession of and remove the display without legal process and legal liability of any nature to either party.

This agreement may be terminated at any time by either party. At termination of agreement, display will be picked up within 5 working days.

The Location percentage of gross receipts is _____ %, payable: _____

Accepted by: _____

LOCATION REPRESENTATIVE
(Manager/Owner)

Accepted by: _____

DISTRIBUTOR

Name _____ Date _____

Address _____ Phone _____

City _____ State _____ Zip _____

19. Location Agreement.

AGREEMENT

Licensee: _____

Licensor: _____

Licensor's Business Address: _____

Location in Premises: _____

Commission to Licensor: _____

Business Phone No.: _____ Pay Phone No.: _____

AGREEMENT made this _____ day of _____
by and between Licensee engaged in the business of installing, maintaining and servicing coin operated pay telephone systems,

and _____ /dba/ _____ hereinafter, referred to as the "Licensor", for the period of five (5) years from the above date.

LICENSEE AGREES TO: [a] supply the leased premises with a coin operated telephone system, [b] service the equipment and keep same in repair at it's own expense during the term of this contract, [c] pay phone charges imposed by Telephone Company with respect to the pay telephone. [d] pay the Licensor the agreed commission on the net pay phone income: i.e: gross collections, less tariffs, in excess of monthly phone line charges in consideration for the space provided, Licensee reserves the, right to install, at its option, another coin operated telephone if gross revenues exceed $500 per month. Licensee will be solely responsible for removvmg the coins from the pay phone.

LICENSOR AGREES TO: [a] provide adequate space for the pay telephone system whlch is easily accessible to the general pubic, [b] not install or permit the installation or use of similar equipment at the above mentioned location, [c] refrain from entering into any other contractural agreement relating to coin operated telephone service whether written or implied with any other person, company or corporation whether sale or lease during the term of this agreement, [d] that any sale or transfer of the business or transfer of the business or property shall be subject to all terms and conditions of this agreement upon the new owner assuming the obligations thereof.

THE LICENSOR FURTHER AGREES TO: release to Licensee, all rights and privileges in connection with pay phone management at the aforementioned address. The authority released to Licensee at this time would include but not be limited to complete management of [a] the removal or installation of existing phone equipment, [b] information about all line charges and other coin phone business conducted with Phone Co. [c] any other activities in regard to complete management of all pay phones located at the above location.

IT IS FURTHER AGREED: [a] that, this agreement shall be binding upon and shall inure to the benefit of the parties, hereto, their successors and assignes and be subject to automatic renewal on the same terms and conditions as stated for continuous periods of five (5) years unless cancelled by written notice of either party at least sixty (60) days prior to expiration of the period in effect at the time of notice, [b] this agreement contains the entire contract between the parties hereto and its terms may not be modified in any respect whatsoever unless in writing and signed by the parties hereto, [c] that no verbal conditions, promises or compensation were agreed to by the participant and/or their agent, [d] all equipment. fixtures and supplies furnished by Licensee shall remain their property, [e] if Licensee finds it necessary to remove their property, they may do so at their option, thus terminating this agreement. [f] The Licensee may, at any time, sell or assign its interest and rights under this agreement in which event the Licensee shall have no further responsibilities or liabilily hereunder. Any such assignee shall have all of the rights and responsibilities of the Licensee.

This Agreement is effective when signed by Licensor and accepted by Licensee

Licensor: _____   Licensee: _____

_____
Name of business

Agent for Licensee: _____

_____   _____
Authorized Signature   Title

Accepted for Licensee by: _____

_____
Print

_____
Title

20. Telephone Agreement.

Digital Access Communications Statement for the month ending 02/27/91 Issued: 03/15/91

February 1991

Account	Grs Coin	Commissions Earned			Rate	Year to date totals		
		Op.Svc.	Adv.	Coin		Grs Coin	Paid Coin	Paid Op.Svc
	$222.15	$16.53	$0.00	$33.32	15%	$402.80	$51.39	$28.79
	$156.85	$18.53	$0.00	$7.84	5%	$290.60	$7.84	$29.93

62	Total due this statement:	$76.22	Total paid year to date:	$117.94

21. *Verification of Pay Phone Revenue.*

LOCATION LIST

Name _____ Address _____ Phone _____

City _____ State _____ Date _____

The following list of names and addresses are places of business which have signified their acceptance of:

. . . .

NAME	ADDRESS	ACCEPTED BY

1. _____
2. _____
3. _____
4. _____
5. _____
6. _____
7. _____
8. _____
9. _____
10. _____
11. _____
12. _____
13. _____
14. _____
15. _____
16. _____
17. _____
18. _____
19. _____
20. _____

I hereby acknowledge receipt of a copy of this list of locations from my route of . . . .

. . . . with the understanding that no guarantee of profits is made or

implied by the seller, and that all commitments made by . . . .

have been complied with. I am satisfied with these locations and am aware that I may change locations if I should

desire.

Operator _____ Address _____ City _____

Locator _____

I HAVE TOURED THESE LOCATIONS   _____
                                        INITIALS

I HAVE NOT TOURED THESE LOCATIONS   _____
                                        INITIALS

22. Location List.

LOCATION UNDERSTANDING

I hereby acknowledge receipt of _____ locations with the understanding that no guarantee of sales is made or implied by the Locator. I am satisified with the locations and I am aware that, should a location become unsatisfactory in the future, it is my responsibility to change to a location of my choosing. The Company and the Locator will not be back to re-locate your accounts. The Locator can get you started in the business and your accounts will vary in sales. It is your responsibility to upgrade your accounts and to fine tune your business to get the best results from your business.

I have read the above and will do my part to make this business a success.

_____   _____
Signature   Date

OPERATOR_____

ADDRESS_____

CITY_____STATE_____ZIP_____

PHONE(____)_____

LOCATOR _____

23. Location Understanding.

YOU WILL ALSO WANT TO READ: